ANATOMY OF A
SCREENPLAY

Writing the American Screenplay
from Character Structure
to Convergence

by

Dan Decker

Contact:
The Screenwriters Group
1803 W Byron
Chicago IL 60613
773-665-8500

Library of Congress Catalaog Card Number: 98-96303
ISBN 0-9665732-0-X

Printed in the United States of America

Acknowledgments

I'd like to thank those who gave so generously of their time and talent to help this book get to press, especially Carl Marziali, Jessica Bornemann, Christi Nelson, Karen Darr, and Valerie Mrak.

- *To* -

John Nordhaus, who has never failed to
challenge me to go beyond myself,

and

Durrell Royce Crays, whose generosity of
spirit got me from there to here.

Contents

Don'T use Comed
or `MoRé anymore

INTRODUCTION

"If it's so easy to understand, why is it so difficult to do?" was a question put to me just last week during one of my lectures. Like anything, learning to write screenplays is a two step process: first understanding the concepts, an intellectual process which any normal person can do. But then comes the application of the concepts to the blank page, and that's where it gets a little tricky.

This book can be used in two ways: to help the reader come to a critical understanding of how a screenplay works by providing a reliable and consistent set of tools by which to measure any screenplay; and/or as a guide to the application of that knowledge to the writing of a screenplay. The guidelines used are developed for use by writers; the insights are to help the writer understand how to approach the pages. If some of the concepts seem counter-intuitive, it is because they have been developed as a way of understanding how to *get to* what you want, not necessarily what you want.

Writing by "plot," that is, writing events by page counts, trying to shape a story by putting a point here or there, is an external, disjointed, and manipulative approach to what is and must be an organic and natural flow from start to finish: the mainstream American screenplay.

It is often, and correctly, said that character is the most important thing in a movie. This book extends that thinking to show that Character is the ONLY thing in a movie; plot is merely a by-product of who the character is, what happens to the character, and what the character does and discovers.

A Note on first drafts: If you are going to use this book

to write a first draft, you must accept that you'll be writing an initial exploration of your idea. Think of it as a "springboard draft". It's a way to take an idea, work through it and see if it can be a movie. See if you can find a workable Character Structure in the idea.

Screenwriters will tell you that 90 percent of the work is in the rewriting, but you can't get to the rewriting until you have a first draft. So don't expect that you're going to blow the doors off Hollywood with your first draft. Just get to the FADE OUT and see what you have.

A Note on spec scripts: Sometimes I will refer to a "spec script." A spec script is a script written on the speculation that someone will buy it. If you are writing a script that no one has asked you to write, you are writing a spec script. A pitchable spec script is 90 to 130 pages long, but whenever I talk about the length of a screenplay I am going to refer to 120 pages. Properly formatted scripts translate to the screen in terms of one page per minute, on average, so a 120 page script will become, approximately, a two hour movie.

A Note on page counts: When you write a first draft, cover up your page counter so you are free to follow the story as you develop it. A properly formatted screenplay has the proper contours and comes in at the right length all by itself. Page count is not something you force on it.

Chapter One
THE AMERICAN SCREENPLAY
A guide for the perplexed; Structure vs. Formula;
Defining what we do best; Og hunt kill

"A Screenplay is an invitation to a collaboration..."
-Paul Schrader

"A Screenplay is a set of intentions you take to the set"
-Michael Tolkin

"A Screenplay is the haiku of literature"
-Clare O'Donohue

The Mainstream American Screenplay.

Market forces have shaped the "Mainstream American Movie" over the last century into a compact and efficient mode of storytelling. The mainstream American movie has evolved in response to the box office only, therefore the mainstream American screenplay tells a story in a way the universal audience understands. Whether films are done by independent filmmakers or major Los Angeles movie studios, they operate from the same story-telling foundation. They differ only in content.

A Guide for the Perplexed

Human Beings use language and the process of converting everything into and out of verbal symbols as our way of understanding our world. We have never found a civilization anywhere on the planet that does not have language. Interestingly, a sentence in any language requires a noun and a verb. A "person" "does" something. 'He runs' is a sentence. And it is perceived as a sentence, a complete thought, in all human cultures. There seems to be a "instinctive" way of understanding a complete thought built into our brains.

Story is the same as sentence. There is a universal, human way of understanding Story.

A sentence requires two things: something or someone doing something. A Story requires those two things and adds a third: something or someone does something... and it works out. *A person...does something... it works out.*

This is the genesis of what has come to be known as the "three act structure" in movies. What the act structure refers to is:

> Act One: *A Person...*
> Act Two: *Does Something...*
> Act Three: *It Works Out.*

It is the way humans tell stories, there is no other way. You can't do it with two steps and four steps confuses it. No matter how you chop and dice it, put the ending first and the beginning second, setup "multiple persons doing multiple things," put the film in a blender and throw the pieces in the air and cut them together at random, it always comes down to: A person does something and it works out.

Does this mean all stories are the same? All mainstream sentences have a noun and a verb and they are not all the same. All mainstream faces have two eyes a nose and a mouth and they are not all the same... They do share the same *Structure.*

People often confuse the words *Structure* and *Formula*, but the two are not interchangeable. Formula is the product of tired, derivative, insecure writing. Structure is the foundation for all great writing.

Defining what we do best

It is true that you can write anything you want and call it a screenplay, but be advised that in the entire universe of script possibilities only a small percentage fit the definition of what you might call the **Mainstream American Screenplay**. You can write whatever you want if you are not interested in selling, but if you are, you have to pay attention to what is considered *mainstream*.

The definition used here fits everything from G-rated family fare to the darkest of the gritty films. There are at least a dozen variations on the different parts of the definition, (i.e. combining, splitting, etc.), but at no time do the concepts change.

A Mainstream American Screenplay:
tells a *story*
about a *main character,*
in search of an *objective,*
in the face of *opposition,*
with an underlying *theme,*
in a clearly defined *genre*
and an emotionally satisfying *resolution.*

Form equals content

Taking each part of this definition in turn begins to show the writer or the reader how the contours of the final film are determined by the content right from the start. And how the script's content begins on page one in order to achieve the full impact of a great movie.

"...tells a *story*..."

The first story ever told was likely told by Og the cave man about 24,225 years ago when he was standing next to a dead rabbit and his neighbor Barney came out and asked, "Og, what happened?" Og uttered the words: "Og hunt kill."

When Og uttered those immortal words, he told a Story: *someone* did *something* and there was a *result*. If he had said, "Og hunt", that would have been just a sentence, or, "Og kill," is just a sentence. It is not a Story until you say what happened:

(1) a person (2) does something (3) it works out.

A person: OG--the introduction of the Main Character, his circumstances, and the characters around him, comprises the "First Act." Og IS the movie, there is nothing else to write about so if you get to it right from page one you shouldn't take more than twenty or thirty pages to thoroughly exhaust the setup potential.

Does something: Hunt. Hold on this thought for a second...

It works out: Kill. The resulting "Third Act," comes together in the last part of the screenplay, again shouldn't take more than twenty or thirty pages to fully exploit.

If it took 20 to 30 to setup the person of the story, that is, Og, and 20 to 30 pages to say what the outcome of Og's hunting is, that would leave around 60 pages for HUNT, or the "Second Act."

> *Structure, is strictly determined by the finished length of the piece.*

So a mainstream movie tells a story. Because of the 120 page length of the finished piece, a movie tells its Story in a particular structure, that is, about one quarter of the film deals with A PERSON, about one half of the film deals with DOES SOMETHING, and about one quarter deals with IT WORKS OUT.

"...about a main character...

Mainstream American movies tell stories about a central figure, or Main Character, but that statement isn't quite right. The story is not *"about"* the character. The story and the character are one concept. The Story *is* the Main Character: what the Main Character *does* and what happens *to* the Main Character; what's the Main's Objective; why the Main can't get the Objective; who the Main talks to about it, etc.

There is no such thing as "plot" in a movie. Plot is just a byproduct of the Main Character's actions. For instance, you can't have an exciting story with a dull Main Character. When a script is "plotty,." the needs of the plot outweigh the needs of the character, resulting in bad, forgettable movies. Decide who the Main is - and I mean the fully expanded definition of Main Character - and plot happens automatically.

When a movie fades in, the audience immediately starts looking for the Main Character. The audience needs, and wants, to know whose story is being told.

7

The classic definition of Main Character is the character who "undergoes change from start to finish." That definition doesn't necessarily hold water anymore. For instance, a "hero" character usually doesn't undergo any change, but the hero is the Main as far as the audience is concerned. There are lots of ways the audience has of telling who the Main Character is - the biggest star, the one with the most lines, the one on the poster,...

My favorite definition of Main Character is: *the first person to make a decision in the movie.* It is not a perfect definition, but it hits at the core of characterization. The screenplay introduces a person, confronts him/her with a situation and requires him/her to make a Decision - usually a yes-or-no decision. When this happens, the audience falls right in behind the character and begins to follow him or her through the consequences of that, (and every ensuing), decision.

X

Effective
Decision

A tip on the creation of effective Decision: To get maximum Character Drive out of the Decision, the Decision should be to do something that is against the nature of the Main Character as we've come to know the Main.

Everything in a movie is defined through the Main Character. Objectives, Opposition, etc., can't be defined until the Main Character is in place.

"...in quest of some objective..."

The pursuit of an Objective is the single most identifiable feature of the Mainstream American movie. That pursuit represents the core Drive of the film. Objective, in its simplest expression is: The Main Character wants some-thing, some perfect state of being (growth), or has some deficit that needs to be filled (redemption). However, the Main Character must also deal with the reality of his or her everyday life. The difference between the Character's every day life and the Character's Objective, and how the Character chooses to pursue that Objective, is where we spin our tale. Getting from here to there is the Objective Drive.

There is double aspect to Objective. There is the "dream Objective:" that one thing that will make life complete for the Main Character. Then there is the "movie Objective:" the path the Main Character chooses to pursue the dream. It is that path that makes the movie go.

A common mistake among writers is to define the Objective in "soft" terms: the character wants love, accept-ance, etc. Well, all of us seek love, acceptance, personal growth, so that doesn't even need to be stated as an Objective. We will assume all characters want this. The audience needs to know what does *this* Main Character want, right here and now that will help get him/her to the Objective, and how badly does he/she want it. The more three dimensional the better.

The Objective could be another person, or it could be a rare postage stamp, or even the world heavyweight boxing title, but whatever it is, the Objective must be easily under-stood and *visual*.

Objectives almost always have thematic sides, too, the deep unspoken motivation of the character, broadly defined as either Redemption or Growth. This aspect is the subtex-tual, or unspoken, objective that is universally human and universally understood.

The Main Character's quest of the Objective is the cen-

9

tral Drive that compels the reader to keep turning pages and the audience to stay in their seats. It is the central drive element in any mainstream American movie, (Drives are discussed in Chapter Three).

"...in the face of opposition..."

The Opponent is *a person whose own Objective is mutually exclusive to that of the Main Character's Objective.* Opposition is *not* defined as "the bad guy." The Opposition is a person who may be just fine but who has something he/she wants, and his/her pursuit of this just happens to be contrary to the Main Character's pursuit of his/her own Objective.

In order to identify the Opponent in a movie, you must first identify the Main Character and the Main's Objective. Only then can you ask why the Main Character can't get his or her Objective. The answer to that question is: the Opposition.

Does the Opposition have to be a *person*? Yes. You are making feature films, not documentaries. A) the only way the Opposition can change and increase activity is if it is a person, and B) it is always personal.

Opposition is a structural need when writing a story with a single Main Character with a single Objective. When working with episodic narratives, ensemble, or A-B stories, (see Alternative Story Structure, chapter five), the structural need for Opposition diminishes.

Here's why Opposition is a structural necessity: The Main Character sets off in pursuit of the Objective somewhere in the beginning of the movie. The pursuit continues: get it, get it, get it... the pages go by... 30, 35, 40, 45, 50, 55, 60... if this Main Character hasn't gotten whatever the damned Objective is by now the audience is heading for the doors - UNLESS there is a clear, compelling, entertaining reason why the Main Character can't get the Objective. All too often, around 60-75 a script goes to pieces because of inactive or missing Opposition.

"...with an underlying theme..."

theme Theme is generated by the Main Character's personal change from start to finish in terms of Universal Human values or emotions. In other words, it is the Main's path of self-discovery. Therefore Main Character, self-discovery, and Theme are inseparable. One concept.

A strong thematic core is highly desirable in a movie. If the Main is a hero-type who will not undergo any change, then another character in the movie is (or should be) given the thematic chore. This second lead character undergoes the change that imparts Theme.

Look at *High Noon* for example. Gary Cooper is a hero Main Character. He's got to do what a man's got to do. It doesn't matter that his wife, Grace Kelly, is going to leave him if he fights the bad guys. She is a total pacifist. However, by the end of the movie, she is right in the thick of the fight biting and kicking and holding the bad guy so Coop can get a shot at him. For better or worse, the theme of the picture was carried by the wife, (the Grace Kelly character) who was also the Opponent in that movie, despite the presence of the bad guys.

Not all movies contain self-discovery, confrontation of values, or personal change. Generally, the more action-oriented, event-driven the movie, the less emphasis on the inner journey of the Main Character. (James Bond does not agonize over whether or not to sleep with a beautiful lady.) As the inner journey disappears, so does the Thematic Drive, and, ultimately if carried to the extreme, the movie collapses into a two-dimensional on-screen comic book. (Which is ok if that's what you want.)

So we see that the classic definition of Main Character in a drama as the one who undergoes the change from start to finish is a good definition, but does not always stand up under the broad range of movie Main Characters. In many movies, it is part of the Main Character that he or she NOT change. When faced with an unchanging Main Character, the clever screenwriter assigns the thematic character changes to another character in the film.

To create a Thematic core and develop a Theme Drive the screenwriter will clearly position the Main Character at the start in terms of universal human values: *what kind of person is this?* By the end of the movie, the Main Character will have come to see the error in his ways, and/or confronted the inner demon, and/or discovered new insights into the human condition, and/or improved upon an already-good self, and will experience the FADE OUT as a different *kind of person.*

Thus the Theme of a movie is always generated by the change in the character from start to finish. Who this Character (usually the Main) *is* in the beginning of the picture, versus who the Character *is* at the end of the picture is the Theme the movie expresses.

For example, in the beginning of the movie, the Main Character is a repressed housewife and at the end of the picture a militant feminist. Or, if in the beginning of the movie she is a militant feminist and at the end of the picture a repressed housewife. Two different Thematic Journeys.

This Thematic core can be at work in any kind of movie, and any screenplay that neglects to develop and resolve Theme is going to be missing an important element.

"...in a clearly defined genre..."

genre

Genre is a word that is frequently misapplied, like: "It's just a genre picture." What that means is it's a picture just like others, or a "formula picture." Genre, more correctly, means what *kind* of picture is it. Which, in turn, means which producer will buy it, how much they will pay for it, who they will cast, what they will spend on production, what the ad campaign will look like, which theatre will book it, which audience will come to see it, which cable *etc* channel will buy it, when the broadcast nets will run it, which overseas markets will be interested in buying the rights for their countries and for how much, and which shelf on the video store your picture will end up on. So I ask you, is genre important?

The writer must understand his or her genre and fully saturate the script with the things that are that genre to the point that a viewer can watch almost any single minute of the movie and know what the genre is. It is not possible to overstate the genre. Can a comedy be too funny? Should we cut some of the jokes out so the audience doesn't hurt themselves laughing? I don't think so.

If you're not sure about genre go to your local video store and rent ten movies from one category and watch till your eyeballs fall out. Get familiar with the elements that cause them to be grouped together. Start with the *visual grammar* used to tell the stories. "A kiss is still a kiss," but if it's on a space ship, or at the old ball park, or in the midst of a car chase, or between two men, you don't just have a Romance movie, you've got a "Romance hyphenated something else" genre, and the second genre you've added will almost always dominate. Romance-Thriller. Romantic-Comedy. Romantic-Drama.

As far as the market is concerned, Genre is the single most important choice you make for your screenplay. Genre is the way we classify our entertainment landscape. It's how books are arranged in a library. It's how producers buy screenplays. It's how they advertise the film. It's how audiences pick their movies. And it's genre that tells the audience what to expect - in fact demand - from the movie.

The categories of genre are not as finely delineated as beginning writers would like them to be. Hyphenated genres abound. New genre develop and old ones fall out of favor. All American mainstream movies have a genre category, and, generally, the more clearly expressed the genre, the better received the film.

Scripts express genre by their visual grammar, their way of *showing* the story's events. Genre should be on your first page and all the way through to the last.

There is no forgiveness here. If the screenplay has no clear genre, the audience will make it up. The audience has its own ideas about genre. The story itself is carried in the audience's collective mind. The screenplay merely evokes it successfully or unsuccessfully. Genre is one of the many tools in the screenwriter's powerful arsenal.

The screenwriter that thinks s/he can get out in front of the audience and lead them where s/he wants is making a fatal mistake. The screenwriter that tries to lead the audience usually ends up with the audience's footprints up his or her back and little money in the till. Those projects fail almost always due to their makers' arrogance, who, in turn, invariably blame the audience for being too stupid to understand their brilliant film. One of the many challenges in screenwriting is to move fast enough to keep ahead of the forward momentum of the audience.

The universal audience, that is, the audience that is looking for the one film, the one genre, that inspires it, does not exist. The wise screenwriter knows this and does not try to write the one-size-fits-all film. Greek theatre is not done much anymore. Shakespeare on film has never really drawn an audience even with rewrites and major stars. Those scripts were written for the sensibilities of their audiences. Their own local "genre" was at work. Our movies today probably would not make sense in the early theatres of Athens. We do not tell stories about the things they wanted to hear about, nor do we tell them in the way they were used to having a story told. The point is, do not underestimate the audience's role.

Each genre has a signature and this will direct your thinking when writing the "genre set piece."

> A genre set piece is simply a scene or sequence that immediately, powerfully, and visually identifies the genre of the movie the instant you see it on screen or read it on the page.

Action pictures have their car chases and explosions; dramas have two people in a room going at it with words; comedies are *funny*, but more precisely, funny in the same way from start to finish, (i.e. low brow, high brow, etc.)

The more clearly and consistently expressed the genre, the better understood the script will be by the buyer, the producer, the director, the audience, and the clerks at the video store, and the more salable it will be.

It is okay to mix genre. Can you have a mystery-romance-western? Sure. But you need to know where to place the emphasis. For instance, is it going to be action-comedy or comedy-action? The answer is never "both."

Either laughs or action scenes need to predominate, or you will appear to be waffling.

Your script will never be all things to all people. Choose a genre and stick with it.

"and an emotionally satisfying resolution"

Movies don't just end. They have four emotionally satisfying resolutions in a genre set piece on the last page. This is American Convergence and is as integral to the American screenplay as Objective. The four resolutions are: the resolution of the Main Character/Window Character relationship; the Objective is resolved; the Opposition is resolved; and the Theme is resolved. Properly done this all happens in the last scene and in a Genre set piece.

Resolution of MC/WC relationship means the script must tell us if they stay friends or not, if they're happy or not, if this is the beginning of a beautiful friendship or one of them has got to die. The audience will have become deeply invested in the relationship between the Main and the Window (See Character Structure, chapter two.) The screenplay has to let us know what happens, happened, and/or will happen to the relationship between these two people.

Resolution of Objective means the script must tell us if the Main gets the Objective or not. It doesn't mean the Main gets it - it means we know. And, somehow, we find that resolution emotionally satisfying. We're ok with it. Bogart doesn't get Ilsa, but we're ok with what happened.

Resolution of Opposition means the script must tell us if the Opposition person lives or dies, wins or loses. We need to know and we need to know at the end.

The trickiest resolution of the four is resolution of

Theme. The script must give us a sense of what is going to happen to the Main *after* the FADE OUT. Does the Main go on to a greater glory or does the Main die in a pool of his or her own blood? That resolution, combined with the change in the character from start to finish, gives us the Thematic (and the writer's) statement on the human condition. This particular person (Main Character) undergoes this particular journey (Objective quest) and in the course of the journey undergoes these particular changes, (thematic journey), and so this, (the future after the fade out), is what is to become of him or her.

If, instead of the beginning of a beautiful friendship, Bogart is shot by the Nazi at the end of Casablanca, you have an entirely different movie. There the resolution of theme becomes more one of: "women are no good; he should have avoided her from the start; there is no redemption; he should never have softened up; he should have taken her and made a run for it..." But if he lets Ilsa's expression of love for him heal his broken heart, and then goes on to a greater glory after the fade out, it is an entirely different picture because of the different resolution of Theme.

These four resolutions all must happen and happen together to end a movie. Once they do, write FADE OUT 'cause there ain't no more.

Protecting your work.

I wish I had a nickel for every time some beginning writer warned me that his work was copyrighted so s/he had nothing to worry about because it was protected. Let me make a few comments here about protecting your writing: In short, there is no protection.

Registration of copyright with the U.S. government and

17

Writers Guild registration are two ways in which you can lay down a paper trail to help later prove that you were the author of record of a specific document on a specific date, which is far from proof that someone stole something from you. The act of registering or copyrighting, by itself, does not provide protection. Neither grants "protection" in the way many writers wish it did. There really is no way to stop someone from stealing what you wrote without going to court and having a judge or jury adjudicate a specific set of circumstances in your favor..

That doesn't mean you shouldn't use the few resources you have. The first way to go about registration is through the U.S. government's office of copyrights. To do this, all the writer needs to do is file a copyright "form PA" along with a copy of the original work, and the US copyright office will keep and file both with a date. If it later appears that someone has "stolen" the script, the writer can file a suit in civil court and use the filed script as evidence of prior claim to the idea. However, the writer will also have to prove that the person being accused was either shown the script, and given the opportunity to refuse to see it, and that it was made clear that the writer wanted to work for the defendant for money. It's often difficult to prove any one of these

NOTE: Please do not use this book for legal advice. Refer any questions you have on this topic to a qualified attorney.

The second method of protection is through a service of the Writers Guild of America. For a small fee, the Guild will file and date a script, just like the copyright office. A writer doesn't have to be a member in order to use this service. However, in the event you feel another writer or producer has appropriated your registered material, the Guild will assemble an arbitration board which will read the allegedly plagiarized script side by side with the script you registered and then make a determination of originality. If the Board finds that some portion of the script in question was lifted from the filed script they will award the original writer credits and whatever fee that goes along with the writing credit they determine should have gone to the ripped-off writer. The Guild is not a court of law and does not award damages. The Guild determines all screen credits for writers. If you go to them, you are filing a credits grievance. But if you do go to court, the screenplay or document you registered with the Writers Guild can be important evidence.

The courts grant that two people can have the same idea at the same time. If you file a claim you must somehow prove that this particular producer got this exact idea directly from you. Not an easy thing to prove when opposing counsel says he didn't and will produce their own documentation to prove their innocence.

The Writer's Guild registration office requires that your title page include the phrase "an original screenplay by." Set up your cover page with the title in caps. Underneath it, write "an original screenplay by" and underneath it, your name. It doesn't hurt to register your screenplay with the Guild before you show it to a potential buyer. Call the Writer's Guild in Los Angeles for information on registration.

Ultimately, the best way to protect yourself from an agent or producer who is inclined to steal from your work is to write the best screenplay version of your idea that anybody in the world can write. Obviously, producers prefer to buy great screenplays and agents prefer to represent great screenplays. A well-documented paper trail through an agency is one of the better ways to jog a producer's memory when he testifies his company never received your script. So writing a great screenplay is the first line of defense.

Secondly, present the script professionally. Agents and producers need to know that a writer is okay, that he or she is not one of the ten zillion kooks that are out there who think they know how to write a movie, but really do not know script from Shinola. Professionals want a professional.

So remember, professional execution and professional presentation are the best ways to protect your screenplay. But go ahead and register and copyright it, too.

Chapter Two
CHARACTER STRUCTURE
Four component characters
The Character Wheel

The organic nature of a screenplay

When you consider that Objective and Opponent cannot be known until you know the Main Character, you begin to glimpse the organic nature of the American movie.

A script is not made up of events that happen here and there. Any approach that advises the writer to make this happen on page such and such, or such and such event is required to end an act or start an act, or that a screenplay goes up and down, is giving plain old bad advice.

An event is not an Event (with a capital E, as in a Drive component of a movie), unless it happens to the Main Character. The character whose Decisions (with a capital D, another Drive component of a movie), move the story is the Main Character, no matter what the writer says. All the bad guys in the world do not constitute Opposition unless and until they get in the way of the Main's Character's Objective.

Page counts, events at act breaks, ups and downs are all by-products of proper Character Structure. Putting the by-products first is writing backwards. That obscures the *movie*, (which is all about the Main Character and his or her actions), from the writer's and audience's vision. In other words, in that kind of formulaic writing, the screenplay gets in the way of movie.

Character Structure is the core of a movie

Character Structure needs to underlie the relationships between central characters, or then by definition, structural characters. Four structural elements or roles are needed to make a screenplay work. These are present in every screenplay. In some stories one character may fill several roles, or one role may be played by several characters (see Permutations of Character Structure, below).

The four structural roles are: Main Character, Objective, Opposition, and Window Character.

Main Character

In the previous chapter I gave my favorite definition of Main Character: "The one who makes the first decision..."

However, American cinema is and always has been shaped by the audience. Keeping true to that American cinema pedigree, we must acknowledge that who the audience perceives as the Main Character, shall be the Main Character. Therefore, it is up to us to structure the screenplay so that our Main Character will also be the audience's. That's sounds silly, but anyone who has read a lot of screenplays knows what I'm talking about. It may be very clear to the writer who the Main is, but no one else can quite figure out why we should be watching any one of the twenty or thirty characters running around and doing things in the screenplay.

The Main Character from the audience's perspective is usually the first character to do something significant on the screen. The Main Character is the person upon whom the audience "imprints," like little ducklings imprint upon the first thing they see out of the shell. If the first character on the screen of the page and the first character to make a decision are the same person, the readers and audiences will perceive that person as the Main Character, regardless of what the writer intends.

Since Theme in a movie is developed by the change in the Main Character from start to finish, the typical script will try to position the Main, (in terms of how he or she relates to other people), in such a way at the beginning so that the change can occur incrementally throughout the movie and the character will end up where the character would ultimately go, considering what's happened to him or her.

Sometimes this presents problems. Actors today often don't want to play people who are less than wonderful, which poses a particular problem for a writer who needs to start with a character who is less than wonderful and change them in the end to someone who is wonderful. So if you are pitching scripts directly to "star" actors with these kind of thematic issues, and the Main Character is, for instance, a compulsive/obsessive neurotic, describe him as "highly focused" or "dedicated." That's just a little pitch humor. The truth is, the top actors, more often than not, look for the most complex, difficult, interesting roles to play.

The Objective

Simply stated, the Objective is what the Main Character is "after." What does the Main want? This can be a person or an object, but it must be understandable in concrete terms. Of course, all humans want to be happy and loved. The question is, how? What exactly does your main character want? Make the Objective as specific as possible because it is absolutely integral to the movie.

It is often best to consider the Objective as a two-step process. The Main has some long term goal, dream, need, want, call it the "Dream Objective." But the Main is also faced with his or her day-to-day life. The movie is about how the Main will get from the day-to-day life to the Dream Objective. The Objective Drive of the movie is in how the Main Character decides to get to the Dream Objective. The chosen path is where the tale lies.

Motivation toward any Objective in a movie, as in life, is based on one of two things: Deficit or Growth. Need or Want. Redemption or Transcendence. I've seen lists of motivations that go on and on, but there are really only two. People are either filling a hole in their lives, in their souls, or they are out to risk and learn through experience in order to grow into an even better person than they already are.

Opposition

Recapping from the previous chapter, Opposition is "a person whose own Objective is mutually exclusive to that of the Main Character." The opponent is always a person. Sometimes this person has others working for him (minions), and sometimes there is more than one Opponent standing in the Main Character's way.

The structural element of Opposition is flexible. The more Main Characters and/or Objectives in a movie (such as in A-B stories, ensembles, or Episodic Narratives) the less the need for active Opposition to keep the movie Driving. (There are only so many pages in a screenplay, and remember, the length of the screenplay is what determines all of structure.)

Opposition is only one element in the Character Structure, and is defined by the Main Character and the Main's Objective. The Opposition is required to have an Objective of his or her own, too, and it's not just to screw up the Main.

Sometimes Opponents take on mythic proportions and a movie seems only to exist to give this Opponent an arena. In an Opponent-driven movie, the audience is barely aware of the Main Character. How many people can remember who the Main was in *Terminator*? Well, ok then, it probably was the robot and it's only fair, then, under our definition of terms, to identify the robot as the Main. Was anyone really interested in Sarah Conner anyway?

Window Character

The Window Character is the person *through whom* we see the changes in the Main Character. A properly constructed Window Character is on the first page, the last page and is there at every critical fork in the road of the Main Character's path from start to finish.

The concept of Window Character goes back to the Greeks and the origins of drama. The Greeks understood that people do not say what they really mean: that the text of their characters' dialog differed from the "subtext," a meaning that transcended the surface actions and dialog in the play. They also knew the audience could not be expected to guess the subtext.

The Greeks solved the problem by providing the audience with a "chorus" onstage which simply *told* the audience what was going on underneath the dialog. It gave the audience clear access to the subtext simply by telling it.

The same need exists in screenplays, but you hardly ever see Greek chorus used in a movie anymore.

If you come a little forward in time to the Elizabethan theater, the playwrights were faced with the same problem. There, they thought nothing of stopping the play and having the characters turn to the audience and explain what they really thought. *Hamlet* has seven soliloquies.

You don't see soliloquies that often in movies, but you might be surprised at how often you do. When a character is trapped alone somewhere s/he must talk to himself so the audience will know what s/he's thinking.

Most of the time in movies today, you will see audience access provided in one of two ways: Voice Over Narration or Window Character.

Voice Over Narration is simply a disembodied voice *telling* you the story from behind the screen. This voice is not part of the drama. In certain circumstance it is unavoidable. A Main Character who is a loner by definition, (i.e. Travis Bickle in *Taxi Driver*, or John Dunbar in *Dances With Wolves*), has no choice but to keep a diary or write letters or have some device that enables him to tell his story.

Except for certain applications, Voice Over Narration is anti-drama and I recommend that it be avoided. If you feel you must use it in your screenplay, do so only in support of the drama, and not in place of it. Never describe how a character feels in narration. Doing so turns emotions into an intellectual exercise. Drama succeeds on the visceral level. Narration is never necessary to tell a story and it is mostly used as a crutch for bad dramatic writing.

You do not need a narrator, a soliloquy or a chorus to access a character's deepest emotions. If you use a "Window Character," you preserve or enhance the drama rather than divert the audience's attention from it.

A Window Character exists as a living breathing person with his or her own Objectives, and as a person the Main Character can talk to. This character is in the entire movie start to finish, and becomes the gauge by which we measure changes in the Main. It is Alice Kramden in *The Honeymooners*. It is Captain Louis Renault in *Casablanca*.

When the Main Character undergoes personal change,

s/he articulates it to the Window Character. Lines like, "I can't never go back to that life again" make more sense if they're spoken to someone who knows what the life was and is.

What makes the Window Character such a powerful tool is that he or she is part of the story, is entertaining in his or her own right, and often plays other roles besides that of the main character's *confidant*. The Window is in every way a living, breathing, three-dimensional character and an integral part of the Character Structure. Ultimately the audience becomes heavily invested in the outcome of the relationship between the Main and the Window and that resolution must be part of the Convergence.

Character Structure

The beating heart of the American Screenplay is Character Structure: a Main Character in pursuit of an Objective, in the face of Opposition, talking to a Window Character.

The screenplay moves past the "set-up" and into the "second act" not as events occur or as the page count mounts, but as the Character Structure develops. The screenplay ends when the Character Structure is resolved in an "American Convergence" (see Chapter Six). The American Screenplay begins, develops, and ends (or converges) according to the Character Structure.

Character Structure in motion
When the Main Character has an Objective and the Opposition Character is *in the movie* (though not necessarily recognized by the audience or presenting any active

opposition to the Main Objective), *the screenplay is in the Second Act.* It does not happen by points or page counts or events happening or not happening. The movie is in its second act when the Main Character has an Objective and an Opposition Character exists, *and at no other time and for no other reason.*

By definition, then, the First Act is the establishment of the Main Character, the Objective, and the Opposition, and Window Character. Again, Character Structure defines the organic whole and all facets are defined in how they relate to or affect the Main Character.

Character Structure, reduced to its absolute meaning, is really an expansive definition of Main Character. The Objective, Opposition, and Window are all defined through the Main. The Main does not exist as a fully expanded movie main character without these other three structural elements.

Let us go back to the first story ever told: "Og Hunt Kill." The 120-page movie made from this story would spend the first quarter establishing the Character Structure: Og, what kind of person he is, what he wants, what happens TO him, what he does. In developing *Og* into a movie, let's say his food source was his vegetable patch and an incoming meteor has killed off all plant life. (Bear with me.) So now Og has to hunt. If we choose an Og whose nature it is NOT to hunt, then we can have a chance at creating some Theme Drive. So we'll select an Og who is a pacifist vegetarian. Now, when a pacifist vegetarian's food source is destroyed, he must hunt or die.

It shouldn't take more than 30 pages to drop the meteor, watch Og and company react, and to let him make his Decisions. It's live or die so he is going hunting, with his neighbor, Barney, who will function quite nicely as the

Window Character.

But now, suppose his wife is a high priestess of the "eat nuts and berries" cult. She will demand, either right away or later on, that he not hunt or eat meat. Now we have some Opposition. Once Og's Objective, <u>food</u>, and his Opposition, <u>his wife</u>, are there, the screenplay is in Act Two, which is HUNT, *regardless of the page you are on.*

That is the organic nature of a screenplay. All structural elements conspire to define all other elements.

Permutations of Character Structure

Is it possible to combine or split these character components? Yes.

Can you have two Main Characters? Yes. When two persons with their own Objectives, Oppositions, and Windows (usually each other) make Decisions that define the course of the movie, they are functioning as a "split main."

Can you have more than one Window Character? Yes. Dorothy had three Window Characters in *The Wizard of Oz*. But a cautionary note is that you only have 120 short pages to work with. How deeply can a screenplay develop multiple Window Characters?

Can you have more than one Opposition? Yes. Splitting opponents will give the screenplay a faster pace: *Romancing the Stone* has two, *Midnight Run* has four distinct sources of opposition. If every time the Main Character turns around, someone is jumping out of the bushes at him or her, the Main will have to make a lot more Decisions and the movie's pace will subsequently increase.

Can you have more than one Objective? Yes. It is very common to change the Main Character's Objective at page sixty in the middle of the movie. In *Schindler's List*, the Main Character's Objective changes right at the halfway point (page 90 in that three hour structure) when he turns from being a profiteer to saving lives.

Can you combine structural roles? Yes. In a typical romantic comedy, the Main Character's Objective is also his Opposition and Window. That is what makes it funny. (It's also what makes the genre difficult to write.)

The important thing to understand is how the four structural roles of Main, Objective, Opponent, and Window make a story work. Whether they are invested in two characters, four, or more is a secondary issue.

Cautionary notes about Character Structure

Avoid making the Main Character his own Opponent (see *Hamlet*). This is the most common question about Character Structure and the most direct route to a boring screenplay. Keep Main Character and Opposition separate. And keep the Opposition human.

Since all of structure is determined by the length of what you're writing, a thirty minute TV episode doesn't really need Opposition to keep the drama interesting. However, in the case of a screenplay, your Main Character is going to be after an Objective by page thirty (or so). You have another ninety pages (or so) to carry on a compelling entertaining story. So the Main Character sets out in search of the Objective around thirty: get it, get it... thirtyfive, forty, fortyfive, get it, get it, fifty, fiftyfive, sixty... if s/he hasn't gotten the Objective by this point the screenplay is getting awfully tedious - UNLESS there is some entertaining, compelling reason why not. That is what structural Opposition is all about.

When there is no Opposition, or when the Opposition becomes inactive in the movie, (such as when the Opposition kidnaps the kid and hides out in the mountains by page 30 rendering himself gone), what inevitably happens is the collapse of the Drives between pages 60 and 90, (more often sooner than later). The Opposition is there to prevent the story from becoming tedious. When tedium sets in right after 60, almost invariably there is no Opposition, or the Opposition has become inactive. If you have a script that is sagging between there, look to the Opposition in the setup, 1-30, or the Opposition's activity, or lack thereof, between 30 and 60. (Refer to Chapter 9.)

Window Character. Lose, remove or do a bad job with the Window Character, and the Main Character will not be understood by the audience, and the entertainment value will be so low that no one will go to see it. You must provide the audience access to the drama. They have to be able to know what is going on inside the Main Character's head. A screenplay is not a novel, which can say "he felt sad." The Main Character must turn to the Window Character and somehow express feelings. Take away the Window and who knows what the Main is feeling?

Objective. Without an Objective, of course, the moment to moment Drive collapses - there is no reason for the Main Character to go on. No Objective=No Opposition, too. The "bad guys" might still be in the movie, but they are no longer acting in opposition to anything. The collapse of Story Drive due to weak or missing Objective will become evident, assuming everything else is ok with the script, usually between 30 and 60, more often later than earlier.

ADJECTIFYING CHARACTER STRUCTURE.

Once the screenplay's Character Structure is in place, we need to understand them, (the four components) on a deeper level.

Let's start with the Main Character.

The writer must always define people as "what" they are in universal human terms. Cynical; obsessive; alcoholic; male chauvinist pig; etc. Notice that these are all connotatively negative. The reason is that by setting forth the underlying description of the Main Character, you simultaneously set forth the theme of the movie. If your movie is to be about something positive in the human spirit, then the Main is positioned as far away from that as possible in the beginning, or set-up, of the screenplay. So it is quite typical that the character will have these sorts of flaws right up front.

Be advised, however, that the American screenwriter better present these flaws in a positive way, or at least in a way that does not repulse the audience. Obsession is better presented as dedication, arrogance as over-confidence and so forth.

A well-crafted script defines the Main Character in outwardly-directed, relationship-oriented adjectives. It tells us how this person relates to other people at the start of the movie, and, in the end, of course, how the Main Character is different. This difference, the Main Character's change from start to finish, is the Theme of the movie. This is how screenplays develop theme *and no other way.*

The more clearly you define the Main Character from beginning to end, the more clearly defined becomes your Theme. This will inform everything you do in the movie.

Which of the following "loglines" do you think most clearly defines the Main Character and thus the Theme of the movie?

It's a story about a broken down gunslinger who takes up with a young kid to kill two cowboys for bounty.

Or how about this:

It's a story about an on-the-wagon former gunslinger with a lot of regrets about the past.

Or this:

It's a story about an on-the-wagon former gunslinger with a lot of regrets about the past who kills a couple of regular working cowboys for an illegal bounty because he needs the money for his kids.

Does the Theme become clearer? Is it becoming deeper and broader? Is it getting to be more compelling? Is it going to guide your decisions all the way through the movie?

Adjectivize the rest:

Just like the Main Character, each of the structural characters should have a clear set of outwardly-directed, relationship-oriented adjectives attached to them. The screenplay should unequivocally evoke them all in universal human terms. After all, every one of your characters thinks they're the Main Character and the movie is about him or her.

Clearly adjectivizing the structural characters will not only enhance the Theme of the movie, but it will also provide the central Entertainment Drive of the script. The structural characters must be chosen to complement each other's personalities. They need not be opposites.

People go to the movies to see interesting people in interesting relationships doing interesting things. Start by positioning these individuals so that they complement each other and support or complicate your intended theme.

Example: Let's turn once again to our movie "Og Hunt Kill." Suppose Og is a *vegetarian pacifist* caveman, and that meteorite knocked out his vegetable patch, which means that if he's going to eat, he's going to have to hunt and kill. Add to that Mrs. Og, who is leader of the nuts and berries cult; neighbor Barney who is a card carrying member of the National Spear Association; and add a life or death Objective about getting food. All of a sudden our ridiculous little story acquires a Thematic core.

THE CHARACTER WHEEL

This is a handy tool for understanding and developing deeper levels in the screenplay relationships. Visualize a circle with four points marked off as on a compass. At the top of the circle place the Main Character. Now ask, "What is he or she after?" Put that Objective at the bottom of the circle. Then ask, "Why can't he or she get it?" The answer is Opposition, so put that name at the right side of the circle. Last ask: "Whom does he or she talk to about it?" That person is the Window Character, so write that name on the left.

Now add expanding concentric circles going out from the center.

Let me press the point of Character Structure here just a bit to show how this works for the writer.

Going through each Structural Character in turn, place each name at the top of the circle and ask the same questions you asked of the Main. Place the names of the answers in the same positions on the wheel, as you build, level upon level. In a well-structured American Screenplay, the same names keep coming up over and over as one's Opposition is another's Window, etc. etc. You can have as many layers, or rings, as you have characters in the script.

Using the character wheel pictured above, let's take *Casablanca* as an example.

The Main Character is Rick Blaine. He goes at the top.

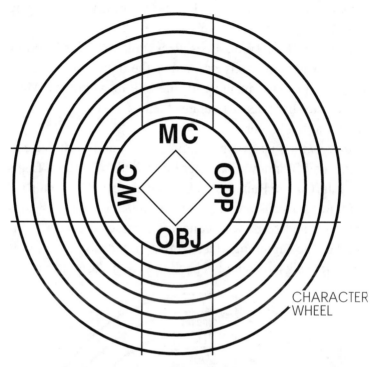

CHARACTER
WHEEL

Next question: What is Rick after? He makes a point of being after nothing until SHE shows up. Once Ilsa, (Ingrid Bergman), walks through the door of the cafe, Rick becomes a different person. He has something he wants now. Ilsa goes in the Objective spot at the bottom.

Next question: Why can't he have her? Well, she's married, that's why. So Rick's Opposition character is Victor Laszlo (Paul Henreid). Take him out, and she's Bogie's. But how can Victor Laszlo be the Opponent/ antagonist, when he is the most noble, the most wonderful, kind, strong, brave, valiant guy in the movie. But yet, he's the "bad guy." If he were anything less, he would be worthless as Opposition; she could just leave him. The greater the person he is, the greater the Opposition he presents to Rick. It is a common mistake to think that the Nazi, Major

Strasser, is the Opposition. He's not because he has nothing to do with Rick's Objective.

Last question: Who does Rick talk to? The Window Character is most easily defined as the one who is there in the beginning and in the end, the one to whom the Main spills his or her guts, articulates themes, and underlines the subtext to the audience.

Casablanca has, perhaps, the clearest and most perfectly executed Window Character I can think of in Capt. Louis Renault (Claude Rains). It is Louis who says, "Oh, but Rick never joins his customers...." It is Louis to whom Rick talks when Ilsa and Laszlo are gone and Strasser is dead: "...this could be the beginning of a beautiful friendship." It is Louis who Rick talks to about his background, his aspirations, his

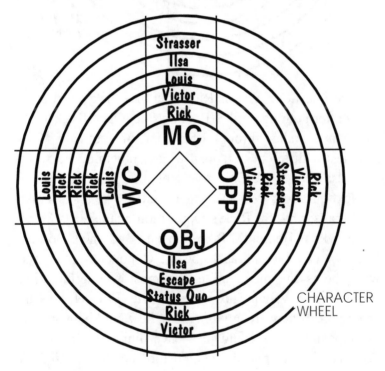

CHARACTER WHEEL

inner humanness. Without argument, place Louis on the left of the wheel. Sam certainly does provide windowing, especially in the Paris flashback sequence, but Sam does not make it to the end of the movie. Sam is not there at every critical junction the way Louis is.

Now, start a new layer.

Make Victor the Main Character. Put him on the top spot. For argument's sake, what does the movie look like if we view it from his perspective, with him as the Main Character? What is he after? He is clearly after the Letters of Transit. That is why he has come to Casablanca in the first place. So put that at the bottom of the circle. In this case the Objective is not a person.

Why can't he get them? Rick won't give them to him. Put Rick on the right as Victor's Opposition.

Who does Victor talk to about this? Ilsa and Rick both. Really Rick more, put Rick on the left.

Next level. Take your pick... Put Louis on the top, he's now the Main. What is he after? Louis is fighting to hold onto what little power he has as Prefect, which means graft and corruption, money, privilege, women... put his status quo on the bottom as his Objective.

Who's threatening Louis' Objective? You can argue that it is Victor because his presence has brought the Nazis, but that's indirect. How about Strasser, who, even without legal authority, can take over the town if he wants to. If you got rid of Strasser, Louis wouldn't care about Victor or anything else.

Who does Louis talk to? Rick. Without a doubt. Put Rick on the left.

Now, put Ilsa on top. What is her Objective? It's not really clear. She seems to be along for the ride, but, I think, if given her druthers, and depending on how romantic you are, her Objective, once she gets to *Casablanca,* becomes Rick. You might say her Objective is simply to escape with Victor and be his faithful wife. This obfuscation may have been purposely built into the story, (but I doubt it). For the sake of avoiding argument put Victor/Rick on the bottom.

Whether her Objective is to leave with Victor or to get back with Rick, both of which she articulates through the course of the film, the Opposition remains the same: Rick. She can't go off with Victor because Rick won't give them the letters. She offers herself to Rick but he won't go for it, his own Opposition (Victor) holding him in check. Rick is her Opposition. Put him on the right.

Who does Ilsa talk to? No one but Rick. How do we know anything about her, except as she tells it to Rick? Remember I said earlier that it is typical Character Structure in a romance to have the Objective, Opposition, and Window be the same person? Well, here it is again. Put Rick in as Window on the left.

Shall we put Strasser on top? Go ahead and work it through on your own.

As we get into the outer layers of the wheel, the first part to fall away or lose focus will be Opposition. That makes sense. Opposition is the most disposable part of character structure.

Remember, stories less than 60 minutes long can work just fine without Opposition because the Objective pursuit can be resolved before the story gets tedious. When you don't have to sustain drama very long, such as in shorter stories, episodic narratives, A-B stories, or ensemble pieces, the structural need for Opposition goes away.

The next to fall away will be Window Characters, and properly so, because less developed people will have less to reveal.

***Og Hunt Kill* gets a Character Structure.**

Who's the Main Character, what does he want, why can't he get it, and who does he talk to about it? Og is the Main. He wants food for himself, his family, maybe the whole tribe. His wife refuses to give her OK for him to kill.

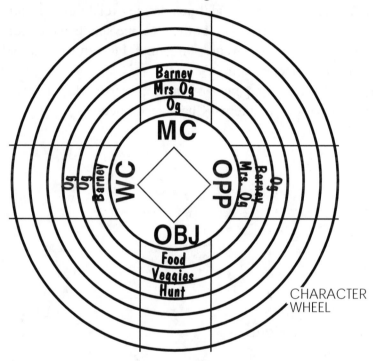

CHARACTER WHEEL

She is the Opposition. He talks to his Neighbor, Barney, about it. Barney is Og's Window.

As the Character Structure develops, Mrs. Og wants food, but not meat. She wants Og to get food but not to hunt. Says she'll leave him if he hunts. Barney, on the other hand, is doing his best to get Og to go hunting with him. They both talk to Og about everything. So if Mrs. Og were the Main, Barney would be her Opposition and Og her

Window Character. If Barney were the Main, Og Hunting is his Objective and Og's own resistance to the hunt makes Og Barney's Opposition.

I am reducing this to an absurd extreme to make the point that there are four functions of drama: Main Character, Objective, Opposition, and Window Character. The four functions are defined as they relate to the Main Character. You can think of them as one single expression. "It's a person, who wants something, but can't get it, and talks to someone about it."

No matter what kind of movie, if it works, it works because it has an internal Character Structure.

Chapter Three
DRIVE STRUCTURE
Second Act Drives
Creating and Controlling The Drives

A "Drive" is something that keeps the reader turning pages and the audience in their seats from minute to minute. It can be developed in any number of ways, and there are a number of distinctly different kinds of Drives. A movie can have a lot of Drives running at once or it can operate on only one Drive.

The six most common drives in a screenplay are:

Objective Drive — *Pg 48*
Story Drive — *Pg 43*
Character Drive
Theme Drive
Genre Drive
Entertainment Drive

Keep in mind that Drive can be created of whole cloth, totally specific to an individual movie. Anything that makes the audience hang in counts as Drive. I was standing on the street one night waiting for a friend and found myself watching a video in the window of a hair salon. Some beautiful model was having her hair cut. I watched as the scissors of the stylist slice through her hair, each cut creating a new angle that was recut again. My friend finally came, but I found I wanted to watch this tape a little longer: it had developed Drive for me as I watched the hairdo slowly unfolding.

Not all screenplays use all Drives. Not all screenplays use the Drives they do use in equal proportion. Often people will talk about a "Character Driven" piece versus a "Story Driven" piece but these two Drives are not mutually exclusive. A script can have Character Drive and Story Drive at the same time.

Event and Decision → DISCOVERY *

All things in a movie are defined by how they relate to the Main Character, or, more accurately, by what aspect of the Main Character they represent. We can say that *everything* that happens in a movie will either happen TO the Main, or happen as a result OF something the Main does. *TO or* *result of*

In other words, let's separate out everything that happens in the movie by whether it is under the control of the Main Character or not under the control of the Main. This is an extremely important distinction because these two different kinds of things that happen create two very different kinds of Drives.

'TO' *EVENT* — If something happens TO the Main Character, or not under the Main's control, call it an "EVENT." If something happens as a result OF the Main, or is under the control of the Main, call it a "DECISION." *result of — DECISION*

Event and Decision are the structural aspects of Story Drive and Character Drive respectively. And it is a simple formula: the more Events confronting the Main, the stronger the Story Drive. The more Decisions made by the Main, the stronger the Character Drive.

Any movie will be set into motion by significant Events and/or Decisions. For the purpose of separating out these significant elements, let's call the major Event that propels the movie the CAUSAL EVENT, and the major Decision that put the character on track the FATEFUL DECISION.

These are major Drive Structures elements and are always associated with the First Act, or set up, of the movie.

Events and Decisions are also the Beats of a movie. A Beat is defined as *a change in the way the character pursues the same objective.* A movie will not only create Drive from Events and Decisions, but the Beat and Sequence structure, which is the overall pace of the movie, totally depends on them. (See chapter seven.)

There is a third kind of thing that can happen in a movie which could be listed under Event but is really a hybrid of Event and Decision. It is called **Discovery**. *Discovery is some fact, clue, or backstory the character finds out through conflict, or through the pursuit of the Objective.* In a mystery, the Beats of the story will go from clue to clue, or Discovery to Discovery. It will usually create Story Drive, but depending on how the character gets to the Discoveries, can also greatly increase the Character Drive.

Story Drive.

Story Drive is developed by Event. Events are things that happen in the movie that are *not* under the control of the Main Character. The more Events in the screenplay, the stronger the Story Drive.

The number and importance of the Events used is up to the individual writer and is how the writer controls the Drive for his or her desired effect.

A lot of great movies run only on Story Drive. The *Bond* movies, for instance. James doesn't make a lot of Decisions. He doesn't even get to Decide whether or not to take the case. He just does. Then he goes off and a lot of things happen TO him. He reacts appropriately, beats the bad guy, then gets the girl. Mostly Story Drive. And a great way to tell a movie. There is not a lot of self-discovery or battling of complex motives involved in making the difficult Decisions, but nonetheless it's two hours of fun at the movies.

Character Drive.

Character Drive is developed the opposite way from Story Drive. Character Drive is developed by the things that happen in the movie that *are* under the control of the Main Character.

A Decision occurs on the page when the Main Character is faced with a choice. The direction of the movie will hang on the Decision the Main Character then makes.

Once the Decision is made, the audience falls in step with the Main Character. Decision gets the audience personally invested and committed to the Main Character and to the outcome of his or her Decisions. They will follow the Character from minute to minute to see what the result will be, thus creating Character Drive.

For a Decision to be even more interesting to the audience, it should not be one that the Main Character would normally make or that he or she can easily make. Therefore, the more contrary to the Main Character's nature this Decision is, the more bounce you are going to get out of your Character Drive.

Meaningful characters are on some path of self-discovery; and a movie will construct some inner struggle to go along with the outer struggle. How well the writer crafts Decisions will determine how the audience perceives the Main Character and whether or not they will still be in the theatre to see what happens to him or her in the end.

Just as in Event/Story Drive, the Decision/Character Drive must be established as soon as possible in the screenplay. Failing to do that will cause a sag between pages 30 and 60 in that Drive (see story diagnostics chapter ten).

Theme Drive

Theme is, if you remember from the previous chapters, the change in (usually) the Main Character from start to finish in Universal Human terms. When the starting point of the Main's character or personality traits is defined clearly (and I mean unmistakably), and the changes in the Main are seen happening as the story unfolds, the audience will watch from minute to minute to see these changes occur and to follow how they work themselves out. That is Theme Drive.

As in the case of all Drives, the Main Character's personality must be clearly defined in the beginning of the movie. The Theme Drive will develop thereafter as the Main changes. The more strongly and clearly these personality features are defined at the outset, the more room the writer has to take the character through clear changes, and the greater the value of the Theme Drive.

That which causes the Main to do the things that bring about the character change is often called Motivation. Motivation invariably boils down to one of two things: either deficit or growth.

Genre Drive.

Genre: *the visual grammar with which you tell your story*. It is the way we understand the universe of movies. When producers look for movies they usually shop by Genre. Genre will determine who buys the screenplay, how much they will pay for it, how much they will spend on production, how the distributor will release it, how much they will spend on advertisement, and, ultimately, who will come to see it.

The audience that comes to see the movie brings with them expectations of the pacing and the visual grammar they've seen before in this genre. If you say you have written an action picture but there are no big Events, no car chases, none of the "visual grammar" of the Action Genre, you have failed to write an Action picture.

When you walk into a video store what do you see: Adventure; Drama; Comedy; Sci-Fi; Western; etc. etc. But, of course, the same is true in book stores, supermarkets, hardware stores... It is simply a human way of looking at the world. Resist genre at your own risk.

Let me argue the case for Genre as Drive. People choose their movies by Genre. They come to see the *kind* of story the screenplay tells. They often know what is going to happen. Does anyone who goes to see a Romantic Comedy, for instance, ever for a moment doubt how it will end? Same with a sports movie.

There is a sheer pleasure in genre, the visual grammar of what you are seeing, that keeps you watching from minute to minute, quite above and beyond what the Story, Character, and Theme Drives are doing. It's not just one of the things you came to see, it is *what* you came to see. It can actually carry the entire movie in the absence of all other Drives. An example of this might be the Western *Tombstone* or the war movie *Saving Private Ryan*.

So how is Genre Drive executed? This Drive does not develop over pages. It is developed in the *look* and the *words* of what is on the screen, repeated over and over again, in each moment. The more Genre Set Pieces, or genre moments, you put on the pages, (if it's a western, give 'em the steaming road apples, the six guns, the shootouts on main street...), the stronger the Genre Drive, and the more delighted and Driven the audience. The audience should be able to look at the movie for two minutes *anywhere* from start to finish and know what your Genre is. It should be on the first page, last page, and every page in between.

Entertainment Drive

As carefully as we study every little element that goes into creating a great screenplay, we cannot forget the reason we are here, the reason a movie exists, is to entertain. The value of Entertainment can create its own Drive. So how is it done? How do you define Entertainment?

People go to the movies to see interesting people in interesting relationships doing interesting things. It is the unique combinations of, primarily, the Structural Characters and Objective that entertains and compels the audience to watch from moment to moment, quite apart from the other Story, Genre, Theme, and Character Drives.

A movie can have this as the only functioning Drive. Take *Home Alone*, an extremely successful comedy. Ask anyone what was it about. They'll say something like, "a little kid has to protect his house from two bumbling robbers." If you look at that film you will find the attempted burglary is about 12 minutes long. No one remembers the rest of the film, the lonely neighbor, the polka band, yet it is a worldwide favorite because of 12 brilliantly entertaining minutes. This is an example of Entertainment Drive being so strong it carries the entire movie.

The screenwriter must choose people to populate the movie based on how they all fit with each other, on what the Objective of the Main is, and on what the Theme is intended to be. In *Casablanca*, for instance, we have Rick (Bogart) who is a cynic; Victor (Henreid) who is noble; and Louis (Claude Rains) who is an opportunist. This is not an accident. You couldn't get more complementary personality traits and this is the genesis of Entertainment Drive.

The crusty old prospector and the Sunday school marm going down the river on a boat together gives you more entertainment bounce that two crusty old prospectors or two Sunday school marms. I'm not saying to make your characters opposites, I'm saying make them complement each other in a way that is somehow appropriate to the movie and the Objective.

Objective Drive.

I've saved the biggest for last. Objective Drive is so fundamental to the American movie that I hesitate to even list it as a Drive. Objective Drive is what the Main Character "wants." As discussed earlier, this is usually a two-step process: there is this dream, this goal that the Main seeks, and then there is the specific path the Main chooses to take (Character Drive), or that is externally forced on him or her, (Story Drive), or a combination of each, that leads from where the Main Character is at the beginning to that goal at the end. — the dream

The Main wants to open a coffee shop and settle down, but in order to get the money he must bring in an escaped fugitive. So what is the Objective, coffee shop or fugitive? For the purposes of the movie and the scene to scene Objective Drive of the Main, the Objective is bringing in the fugitive.

A fully-drawn movie Main Character has an Objective. Objective is part of the absolute definition of the Main Character. Main and Objective are one concept. What motivates the Main to pursue the Objective will invariably boil down to either deficit or growth, (see Theme Drive).

Here's a tip to writers: Before the Main Character has

"the" / big Objective, the big one that Drives the movie, he or she already has an objective. In other words, when the movie starts the Main already has some reason for getting out of bed. A common error in movies is starting with a Main Character who is basically waiting for something to happen, who doesn't really want anything until the big moment comes when the writer brings in "the" Objective. The reader spends twenty or thirty pages watching the Main Character go window shopping, turning off alarm clocks, going to parties and funerals, etc.

Og Hunt Kill develops the Six Drives:

Let's apply some of this Drive Structure to our movie *Og Hunt Kill.*

Let's do **Theme Drive** first. Theme is derived from clearly establishing who the Main Character is in terms of universal humanness right up front. Og is a pacifist. A gentle vegetarian, caveperson, horticulturist who picks food from the garden outside his cavehouse. Og's universal adjectives: Pacifist Vegetarian.

Now that Og is a pacifist vegetarian, the story is "a pacifist vegetarian caveman hunts and kills," all of a sudden we have a thematic core. Simply by using a couple of adjectives, we can tell Og must confront his values and come to terms with himself. He is on a path of self-discovery. The audience is aware of this and will pick up on it at once. They will be compelled to watch as this man changes from minute to minute.

On to **Story Drive:**

A meteorite falls to earth outside his cave. What could be more clear, and more clearly outside the control of the Main Character? This is an Event and will generate the Story Drive.

49

So there it is. Causal Event. A meteorite hits the ground. Og's wife, awakened from a sound sleep, says: "Og. What was that?" Og goes out to see that the meteorite has blasted his vegetable patch, and everyone else's too. His food has been wiped out. As a matter of fact, the event is so cataclysmic it's wiped out all the vegetation. Og and his wife are in deep trouble.

Next, **Character Drive**:

Og's neighbor, who is a hunter, a pleasure killer (his adjectives), comes to Og to ask him if he would like to go hunting. Og has a decision to make. We have established him as a committed pacifist vegetarian. But his family is hungry. "Yes or No, Og?"

What will be Og's decision? In a successful movie, "Decision" is almost always "yes." It is hard to get Character Drive started on a "no."

So, Og has decided to hunt. He is not really going to do it, is he? Is he really going to risk losing his wife for a mastodon steak? Omigod. Turn the page, quick. Character Drive has kicked in now, on top of the Story Drive created by the meteor.

Last, do not forget **Genre Drive**:

We haven't yet decided what *kind* of movie we want *Og Hunt Kill* to be. Should we make it a Drama? An Action/Adventure... How about Romance? No. Not right. A Comedy with Jerry Lewis playing Og? Perhaps. Whatever you decide, know your movie's genre and stick to it.

You can hyphenate genres and have an action-thriller-comedy-drama-western. However it usually better if you can pick one, or at most two so you only use one hyphen. If your genre is not clear you are not going to find anybody mainstream who wants to buy it.

Suppose we pick Drama as the genre for *Og Hunt Kill*.

The essential set piece of Drama is two people who want something from each other that they cannot get, and who will try to get what they want from each other primarily by talking. Compelling drama is hard to do at any time, but in *Og Hunt Kill*, it would even more difficult..

The first time Og wakes up to the problem, he and his wife must talk about it in terms that suit the genre of drama. They need something from each other that they cannot get. He wants her permission to go hunting and she adamantly wants him to find another, bloodless, solution to the food problem.

If Og's wife is going to form the Opposition, we will want her to be in some significant way complementary to Og, while at the same time having an agenda that works in opposition to Og's. So we make her the priestess of the local nature cult: dedicated anti-violent, non-blood eaters of nuts and berries who would rather die than eat the flesh of their woodland friends. She needs Og to help her find another way to get food. She cannot do it without him.

We have now positioned the Character Structure of *Og Hunt Kill* to suit the intended genre of drama. Or, more accurately, the Character Structure will now do what the writer wants from the first time the Main is on the screen to the final convergence of the Structural Characters. It will be as Dramatic, as needs-in-conflict, as it can be. The Drama lovers in the audience will stay glued to their seats.

Objective Drive is simple. Food.

The Dream Objective is survival and getting back to normal. The Movie Objective is food.

Lastly, we have **Entertainment Drive**.

Who are these people and what are they doing? The Character Structure, so far, is

Og as Main

Food as Objective
his Wife as Opposition
his Neighbor as Window

So what is it about these three people and that particular Objective that makes this an entertaining movie? Main Character, Og: obliging, vegetarian, proud breadwinner. Wife, Opposition: militant pacifist, loving wife; Neighbor, WC: pleasure killer, survivalist.

We have now created a blueprint for the American Screenplay. We have a Main Character in pursuit of an Objective in the face of Opposition talking to a Window Character, with clearly defined thematic adjectives for all characters, Events occurring, Decisions being made, and all of this happening in scenes and sequences that are being told in a clear visual grammar.

Chapter Four
STORY STRUCTURE
Defining Motion Picture Structure
The Elements of Story
When Story Goes to the Movies

An American Screenplay tells a story. What does this mean exactly?

The first full-time screenwriter was probably Roy L. McCartle. He was hired in 1898 by Biograph Studios on his boast that he could write ten "photoplays" a day. In those days a movie was not what it is today -- there were no edits. Actors/actresses would act something out in front of a camera in real time and that was the whole movie.

Ian Hamilton's *Writers in Hollywood, 1915-1951*, reprints a McCartle photoplay called "The Pretty Stenographer" or "Caught in the Act." It goes like this:

> "An elderly, but gay broker is seated at his desk dictating to his pretty typewriter. He stops in the progress of his letter, bestows a kiss on the not unwilling girl, and as he does, his wife enters. She is enraged taking her husband by the ear, she compels him to get on his knees. The pretty typewriter bursts into tears. The End."

The first moviemakers would go down to the local "legit" theater and get a couple actors to pantomime the script. They would take the film, process it, make a bunch of copies, and ship them around the country to be played in the nickelodeons, the neighborhood theatres of the day. The audience would come away dazzled that the pictures actually *moved*: "Did you see *that*?? It looked so real."

Today, audiences come out of the latest whiz-bang zillion dollar grosser saying: "Did you see that?? It looked so real."

Ah, we have come a long way.

The most important principle of motion picture structure is this: your finished script has a predefined length, 90 to 130 pages. We usually use 120 pages as a convenient norm. Knowing the approximate finished length of your screenplay before you start is an enormous piece of information. It is confining but liberating at the same time.

You already know, for instance, that at page sixty you will be halfway through your story. Your Main Character better be halfway through his/her story. If the script hasn't reached halfway around page 60, the screenplay is in trouble. As self evident as that sounds, many writers find it terribly elusive.

The length of the story determines "what happens where" in the course of the screenplay. That, and the fact that certain things *must* happen in order for the pages to even *form* a story (a person, does something, it works out). Fixed length and fixed story requirements are the pillars of story structure.

The fixed length of a screenplay is a luxury that novelists do not have (another reason why novels do not translate well to the screen). Novelists can write and write and write. Such a thought is frightening to screenwriters: If they did not know what their finished length was going to be, how would they structure their story? For screenwriters it's easy, and it is also unavoidable. Halfway is halfway. Halfway is page 60. And, as always, *there is no other way,* that is, there is no other halfway. The logic of structure is unrelenting.

Extend this "halfway" thinking to its fullest logic. 30 is one-quarter. 120 is the end. 90 is three quarters. A lot of new writers want to resist the tight logic of Story Structure.

Fixed story requirements are also either a luxury or curse, depending on the writer's taste and disposition. In an American Screenplay, a person / does something / and it works out. You know the screenplay is going to be 120 pages long. The audience looks for the Main Character and what he/she wants right away. Establishing Character Structure defines the start of the story and the movement into the second act. The clever screenplay gets right on it, knowing there is nothing else that is the movie. If the script is not laying out Character Structure from page one, what else is it doing?. Any script will take about 20 to 30 pages to lay out the Character Structure and, hence, enter the second act, (the "does something" part of Story).

Conversely, the movie will end when the Character Structure has been converged (see chapter six). Convergence takes no more than 20 or thirty pages to execute. You don't have to be a mathematician to understand why second acts in movies are around 60 pages long. That's what's left when you start with 120 pages and know the setup and convergence together will require about sixty pages max.

The quarter point

The first twenty or thirty pages of the screenplay develops the Character Structure and Drive Structures of the movie. *No where else.* Once the Main, the Objective and the Opponent are in the movie, the movie is in the second act. I call this the "O/O," (pronounced "oh'n'oh"), for "Objective and Opposition."

The midpoint

The page 60 MidPoint (MP) in a movie is the most important benchmark in the entire Story Structure. It is the heart of the story, the balancing point, the tallest pole in the tent, the way the writer nails the story to the table. The successful screenplay will never find itself without a clearly understood MidPoint.

The Midpoint defines the proportions of the story with greater authority than page 30 and page 90 do. For instance, say for sake of argument the movie is to be a love story: boy meets girl in the beginning, stuff happens in the middle, and boy marries girl in the end. What's halfway? What will the page 60 be?

In the case of this love story, if you determine that Boy will propose to Girl on page 60 you have a fundamentally different story than if Boy and Girl share their first kiss on page 60. The proportions of the story are vastly different, even though the story has the same beginning and ending. Even if someone were to describe the movie, the description would be the same: Boy meets Girl, they fall in love, the get married. Leave that description to the ticket buyers. Know that from the writer's or analyst's point of view, it's really all about page 60.

So how do we define a MidPoint? MidPoint can be defined in both Theme and Story terms.

Take the thematic journey of the Main Character -- who he or she is in the beginning versus who he or she has become at the end -- and ask, what's halfway? What is the first action the Main does to give an indication of where he or she is heading?

MidPoint is also defined in Story terms, or, what is the Main Character's Movie Objective from start to finish and what would be the logical halfway point of that journey?

This is executed in many ways. It can be a change of Objective. The MidPoint can also be the first time the Main recognizes the Opposition. Or, it can be some action that has the result of taking away options from the Main Character, forcing him or her on a collision course with the conclusion.

It's a point of no return. It's where the movie shifts from diverging possibilities to converging possibilities.

Page 90

From page 30 or so the Main Character has been pursuing an Objective. As in life, the Objective may have changed, or the Main Character may have been fighting Opposition. After about an hour, at the MidPoint, some things have developed in the pursuit of the Objective to put the Main Character on a collision course towards its inevitable convergence.

After passing the MidPoint, the Opposition is at its most active. Remember, a movie will collapse right here if there is no opposition. Inevitably, the Opposition will slowly gain the upper hand, or the Main Character's struggle will intensify to where s/he just doesn't seem able to achieve the Objective.

At that point, typically page 90, as in life, there are three possibilities. Yes, no, and maybe.

Option 1: The Main has achieved the Objective. If that occurs by page 90 the movie is over right there and all that follows is anti-climactic. This ought not happen.

Option 2: The Main no longer cares about the Objective.

If that's the case, then neither does the audience, and the movie is dead.

Option 3: The Main is in such a position that s/he cannot possibly get the Objective *unless s/*he takes some decisive action. Now, the story gets the kick into the convergence it needs. Page 90 becomes the **Lost Point**, (LP), in the movie: "the place at which the Objective is lost from the Main Character's perspective." It must be this way to drive to the convergence *and no other way.*

Story Line -- summing up structure in one sentence

A Story Line is one sentence in a cause and effect statement. The sentence begins with a causal word such as: when, since, after, or because. "When" is a good one to use. Then the sentence must have a Main Character Adjective. Next, add the Event or Decision and the Objective, and you have a Story Line.

The interesting thing about a Story Line is that once you understand the inevitability of structure, you can look at the sentence such as, "When an embittered drunk's lost love shows up, he tries to win her back," and know on what page the events will be happening. You know that the lost love showing up is the Event and will happen on or before page 30.

Act 1: When an embittered drunk's lost love shows up, (up to page 30)

Act 2: he tries to win her back (after page 30).

And when does Ilsa show up in Casablanca?

NOTE: Developmental exercises like Story Line are the

most difficult and the most powerful tools available to a writer developing an idea. They are powerful because with the merest change of a phrase or a word, you change the entire theme, genre, character structure, beginning, ending, anything and everything. For instance, instead of "it is an Action-Adventure about..." make it, "it is a Drama about...." That is an obvious example, but as you can see, before you've written the first word you have already rewritten the whole script.

Og Hunt Kill gets a Story Line.

Let's use Og for an example. Og is the Main Character and we know what he's going to do: hunt for food. The story line would go like this: "When a meteor comes to earth and wipes out his food source, a vegetarian pacifist cave man must hunt."

The Story Line suggests all sorts of wonderful things. In the beginning of the movie we are going to find who he is. He is going to lose his food source and he is going to be forced to hunt. The meteor will hit right away, probably on page 1. He will be forced to hunt around page 30. The hunt will go on for an hour, until page 90. Og will face his pacifism and somehow come to terms with himself on that subject when he makes his decision to kill or not kill the animal. It is a drama. All this from the Story Line.

The Story Line is an extremely useful, if bare, statement of your movie. It does not need to include Opposition, or Window Character. Genre is usually implied in the way you say the sentence (for example, if the sentence is funny you can expect a comedy). You can always expand the story line by adding Opposition, Window Character and so forth.

"When a meteor comes to earth and wipes out his food source, a vegetarian pacifist caveman goes hunting with his neighbor over the objections of his pacifist wife." And now to that line apply the Story guidelines: By page 30 the hunt has begun and Og will hunt for the next 60 pages until he reaches the point where, from his perspective, he will never get any food. He then must take the compelling action that will overcome the problem and put him on the path to the eventual convergence.

Although you can, there is no need to put the ending in the story line. Movies end by resolving or converging the Character Structure: Resolve Objective: Og will either kill or not kill the animal for food; Resolve Main Character/ Window Character Relationship: What becomes of his relationship with his Neighbor. Resolve Opposition: The Wife will be involved in the ending one way or another. Resolution of Theme: Og will complete his inner journey and either excel or fall back as a person. (See chapter six for a more expansive discussion of Convergence.)

The Story Line has another use: self-protection. It will help you say what your movie is about without spilling its and your own guts. When a well-meaning friend comes up to you and says, "Oh, you're writing a screenplay. What's it about?", come back with genre, main character and objective in a single crisp sentence and that should have the desired effect of ending that conversation right on the spot. You don't want to stumble and fumble to try to explain what your story is about, or try to talk about what's on your creative mind at the moment, or blurt out your idea only to get an apathetic response that will derail you. You don't want to release the pressure of the story from inside of you by speaking it out loud.

Learn how to say, "it is a comedy about this tough guy who has to take an accountant prisoner." Genre, Main Character, Objective. Or, it is a drama about an alcoholic woman and her uptight husband and how they struggle to try to keep their marriage together for the children. Genre, Main Character, and Objective. Learn how to say your story elements in a story line. Practice it in a mirror so that when someone comes up to you just shoot it at them and change the subject.

PREMISE, THEMATIC JOURNEY, AND MORAL

For the purposes of this brief discussion, let "Premise" mean *the world which is proposed*, for this particular movie. The premise is the "premises" of the story. It is the world through which the Main Character passes on his or her "Thematic Journey." The world remains steady, unchanging, consistent as the Character passes through it and changes. Whether it's the premise of mean streets or Wall Street, it remains the environment from start to finish.

Into this premised world enters the Main Character. This particular *type* of human being, (as described most handily with the outwardly directed, relationship oriented adjective discussed earlier), is going to pass through this premised world and undergo a change. It is that change, the difference between who the Main is in the beginning versus who the Main ends up becoming, that conveys the Theme of the movie and the change itself can be thought of as the Thematic Journey. The world, or Premise stays unchanged, but the Main changes, and that change creates the Theme.

Now "Moral:" As this Thematic Journey takes place, the movie draws to its convergence. One of the four resolutions of the American Convergence is the Resolution of Theme. It means, giving the reader and the audience a sense of what is *going to* happen to the Main after the FADE OUT. This can be thought of as the Moral of the Story. It is the statement that is deduced by the audience from the Premise and the Thematic Journey. This particular world, this particular person, this particular journey... will lead to this inevitable future: greater glory or death; success or failure; get the girl or lose your soul.

Chapter Five
ALTERNATIVE STRUCTURES
A-B Stories; Split Mains; Fractured Time Lines; Episodic Narratives

There is an organic wholeness to the structure of a movie. As individual elements of the film are altered, the entire movie changes its shape. All the various structures of successful movies are variations of the same basic Character Drive discussed earlier.

This chapter will address these questions and more: Can you have more than one Main? More than one Opposition? More than one Window Character? Can the Main be his own Opposition? Can the Window Character be the Opposition? Does the Opposition have to be a person? What if my story has no Opposition?

X *Character Structure* is Main Character, Objective, Opposition, and Window Character.

MC
OBJ
OPP
WC
Character Structure

This represents the straight-ahead narrative story, where a person does something and it works out in a 120 page frame. A Main Character pursues an Objective in the face of Opposition with someone to talk to about it. These elements will give the script a fighting chance to stay interesting, driven, and accessible all the way through.

Can a script have more than one Opponent?

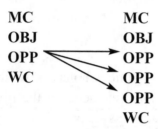

Character Structure with multiple opposition

Multiple sources of Opposition are commonly used to increase the pacing of a Movie.

Examples: *Midnight Run, Romancing the Stone.*

A distinction must be made between multiple sources of Opposition and Opposition's minions. A separate source of Opposition exists when one Opponent can be dispatched but yet the other is still there, operating independently of the former. Notice in *The Wizard of Oz* when the Wicked Witch is killed, the flying monkeys are no longer a threat. The flying monkeys were never the Opponents. The Witch was the Opposition and the flying monkeys her minions.

In *Midnight Run* the Main's Objective of bringing John Mardukas to LA is opposed by Alonzo Moseley (FBI), Jimmy Serrano (mobster), Eddie Moscone through his minion Marvin, and by Mardukas himself as a fourth source of Opposition. Every time you turn around in that kind of structure someone is jumping out at you. Pace increases like mad, which in an action picture is a good thing. An interesting note is that Marvin breaks away from Eddie and actually becomes a separate Opposition, upgrading himself from minion to opponent.

Can you have more than one Objective?

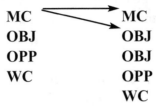

MC	MC
OBJ	OBJ
OPP	OBJ
WC	OPP
	WC

Character Structure with multiple objectives

A change in Objective is what commonly happens at the Midpoint in a script when not forced by Opposition. When forced by Opposition it more commonly happens at page 90. Change in Objective is often used in place of Opposition or in the face of weak or unchanging Opposition.

Example of a single change at MidPoint: *Schindler's List.*

Objective, being the core Drive of the movie, must be carefully and clearly defined and pursued. Two *simultaneous* Objectives for one Main Character tends to split the movie in two.

Multiple Objectives means the Main develops an entirely different dream to pursue; that intangible goal the person drives toward by doing certain actions that constitute the movie's Drive. This is not uncommon. The trick is to keep the audience with the Main as the Objective changes. That is why the Objective will almost always change at the midpoint of the story. In *Schindler's List*, Schindler's Objective is to make money. Nothing else. He is very good at it and, in fact, unopposed in his quest. But at the Midpoint, (page 90 in that 180 minute film), his Objective becomes saving lives.

Multiple Objective is not to be confused with Episodic Narrative where the pursuit of Objective constantly changes but the dream stays the same. And not to be confused with Ensemble or A-B stories where there are multiple Mains pursuing multiple Objectives.

Can a script have more that one Window Character?

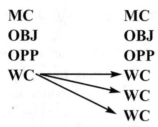

Character Structure with multiple Window Characters

It is true that everything in the movie windows the Main Character: Every character, every location, every line. *Window Character*, however, refers to a specific structural function best executed with a character who is there from start to finish in the movie, and who is there at every critical junction along the way of the Main Character's journey from start to finish. This is not in place of other windowing. Sam, in *Casablanca,* is a good example of a window character who is not THE Window Character. The Main Character and the Window Character form a relationship and that relationship must be resolved at the end. (See Convergence, chapter six.)

The cautionary note on multiple Window Characters is that since there are only so many pages in a screenplay, how many characters can be fully developed within that framework? You could end up multiple with 2-dimensional

Window Characters.

Example: *Wizard of Oz*.

In *The Wizard of Oz* Dorothy acquires her three Window Characters and happily goes with them through every critical junction on her journey. They are all there in the Convergence at the end and her relationship with each is resolved. Even though they are memorable characters and part of American cultural iconography, they don't display a great deal of depth as people. Any script can have two, three, or more Window Characters. Just remember you are writing with a limited number of pages so each additional character means they all get fewer pages, and so, less development.

When the Main changes geographic locations and the Window Character cannot go along, the script must develop a new Window Character in the new location.

Example: *The Lion King*.

In *The Lion King* when little Simba leaves Pride Rock and exiles himself to the jungle, his Window Character cannot go with. Once in the jungle, he meets the wart hog and the meerkat, who become his new Window Characters, and is once again properly windowed. Please note that when Simba returns to Pride Rock, the new Window Characters go back with him so a proper Convergence can be executed. Imagine the movie if the wart hog and meerkat stayed behind.

Can the Window Character also be the Opponent?:

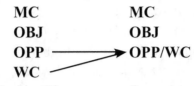

Window Character as Opposition

All Structural Characters can be combined or split.

Often the most entertaining and challenging Opposition characters are the ones that have a close personal relationship with the Main Character.

Example: *Midnight Run.*

In *Midnight Run* Charles Grodin is the Window Character and is also an Opposition Character.

The best example of combining the structural roles in one person is found in the typical Romantic Comedy structure. There, one character becomes the Objective, Opposition, and Window Character all rolled into one.

Example: *When Harry Met Sally.*

Combining in a Romantic Comedy

"What does Harry (Main Character) want? Sally (Sally is Objective). Why can't Harry get her? Sally doesn't want him (Sally is Opposition). And who does Harry talk to about it? Sally (Sally is Window Character).

Yes it's true that Harry and Sally both had other windows played by Bruno Kirby and Carrie Fischer, but as discussed above, everyone in a movie windows, but not everyone is THE Window Character. One of the things that makes the Romantic Comedy genre so delightful, and so difficult to write, is this very construction.

"So what happens if the script doesn't have an Objective?"

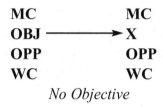

No Objective

Example: *Non-mainstream American films.*
Please refer to the title of this book: Writing the AMERICAN Screenplay, and as pointed out earlier, the MC/OBJ is one concept when you are in the mainstream.

"I saw a movie that didn't have a Window Character."

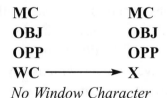

No Window Character

Referring back to the discussion of Window Character in chapter two, the structural function of the Window Character is to provide audience access to the mind of the Main, and to do so in a dramatic way keeping with the art form. There are other ways to provide audience access and in the absence of a Window Character, one or more of them must be provided.

Example: *Taxi Driver.*

When you have a character who by his very definition is a loner, it would be a violation to have him talking to someone just so the audience knows what he's thinking. In *Taxi Driver* the common device of the spoken diary is used in place of the Window Character. This is a compromise with a straight voice-over narration track.

Voice-over narration is almost always misused in movies. Let me say this: *It is never necessary to tell a story.* Once the filmmakers understand that, then the script can start to employ voice-over narration in ways that enhance the story and not supplant it. Voice-over narration is anti-drama, anti-emotional. It works best when used as a framing device or as a bridge in episodic narratives, example: *Forrest Gump* or in the 40's-style movies that were stylistically emulating radio drama, example: *Lady From Shanghai.*

Forrest Gump uses the people on the bus stop bench as a surrogate Window for Forrest. He sits there and tells them each a different, successive piece of his story. His telling of the story becomes a narration track for the film, but the filmmakers had the good sense to shut him up when the big emotional moments of the film came along.

Yes, you can have a movie without a Window Character. In place will be either a character who talks to himself (soliloquy) or a voice-over narration track of some sort.

"Does the Opposition have to be a person?" (That's probably the most commonly asked question in screenplay class.)

Character Structure without Opposition

Feature films are about people. If the structural opposition is replaced by a non-human, such as a mountain, or society, or a god, the impact on the film's structure is profound. This is not to say 'bad.' The resulting story will necessarily be an episodic narrative. An episodic narrative is told by putting together a lot of short pieces of drama, which means smaller, more immediate Objectives. As each Objective is attained, a new one pops up creating a series of five to ten minutes episodes when all added up still equal the pursuit of a larger Objective.

Example: *Apollo 13.*

The Episodic Narrative

Example: *Apollo 13; Forrest Gump.*

An Episodic Narrative story does not take the form of a driven narrative but tells itself in terms of vignettes, more or less related to each other but somehow able to suggest a story and theme. The biggest-grossing drama of all time, *Forrest Gump*, was such a story and, properly done, there's not a thing wrong with it.

In the "standard" structure, there is a Main Character who wants something but cannot get it because someone is in the way. This setup is intended to provide the dramatic potential to carry the Main Character's pursuit the full 120 pages.

The Opposition Character's activity prevents the Main Character's quest from getting tedious. Without an

Opposition, the Main's quest will get tedious *unless* the quest *changes* frequently. The ultimate expression of this structure is the Episodic Narrative.

The main feature of the episodic structure is that no drama needs to be sustained beyond the sequence level: five to ten minutes or so. The need for the structural Opposition character is obviated. Opposition comes in short bursts. *Apollo 13*: every time the story starts to sag, another dial goes haywire and another exciting ten-minute sequence is assured.

In the definition laid out earlier, the script is in the Second Act when the Main Character has an Objective and the Opposition is in the movie. In an episodic narrative, without an opponent, the second act simply begins with the development of the Main Character's first Objective and the commencement of the first episode of the movie. This means the first act will be shorter and consequently so will the third act. (Remember. the third act in a movie is a function of the first act. See Convergence chapter six.)

Multiple Main Characters

There are three ways movies can support more than one Main:

The Split Main.
Example: *Thelma and Louise.*
The A-B Story.
Example: *Fargo.*
The Ensemble.
Example: *Grand Canyon.*

Split Mains

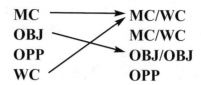

Split Mains become each other's Windows

What's happening here is that two characters are functioning according to the definitions of Main Character, that is, they are both making Decisions that Drive the movie. Their two Objectives are closely related so that their two journeys will take them in the same direction or to the same geographical places. Then two Mains become each other's Window Characters. Each of them can have minor Window Characters if necessary, but those will not be structural.

Example: *Butch Cassidy and the Sundance Kid.*

Or, the earlier example cited was *Thelma and Louise.* I guess it's not too hard to guess what the Split Mains are by looking at the titles. The thing to remember when you set out to write or analyze this construction is that both characters make Driving Decisions and are each other's Window. If one is making Decisions and the other is going along for the ride, or is making lesser Decisions only in reaction to the first character's Decisions, then the construction is not a Split Main.

A-B Story.

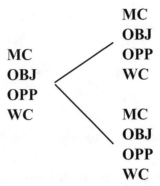

Character Structure is duplicated in A-B Stories

An **A-B Structure** is created by having *two separate stories* that run independently of each other. Sometimes one of the stories will start and finish the movie while the other, the "B" story, will run its course within the "A" story, such as in *True Lies*. Sometimes the two stories will combine into a new third structure to finish on, as in *Titanic*. Sometimes the "B" story will transcend the "A" story and become the ending, as in *Fargo*.

The "A" story cruises along in standard fashion. The "B" story can begin and end anywhere within the time frame of the movie. A "B" story must somehow be related to the "A" story: it will either *mirror, oppose, or parallel* the main story on a character and/or theme level. You must make sure you are dealing with one movie and not two.

The A-B structure is NOT a split Main. In a split Main, both Main Characters are in the same story. In an A-B structure, at the outset you will find two Main Characters in two separate stories (two Mains with two unrelated Objectives). They can combine later. There is no rule that says the "B" story cannot end at the same time as the "A's" story. Caution is advised, however. Make sure the characters, objectives, and their actions have been introduced and developed clearly enough so that when they are intertwined the audience can follow the segue from one to the other.

The Ensemble

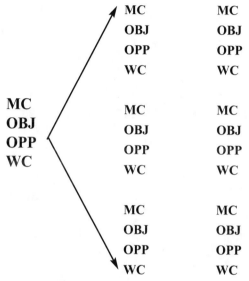

The Ensemble Structure

The Ensemble structure is an extension of the A-B Story into numerous Mains and Objectives. The **C,D,E... stories** have their own mini Character Structure and tell their own story, develop their own theme, etc. The various stories can happen at the same time, in sequence, or all chopped up.

As the little stories increase, the number of pages each sustains decreases as does the structural need for Opposition. The little character structures plotted out above can delete the OPP.

the ENd

Chapter Six:
AMERICAN CONVERGENCE
Four Resolutions

The ending, or third act, of an American movie is a mirror of the set up, or first act. A movie ends with the same Character Structure with which it starts. A movie tells one story. That means one set of characters from start to finish. That means the movie ends by resolving the Character Structure with which it starts. It can be said, in that way, that movies end the same way they begin as in the diagram below.

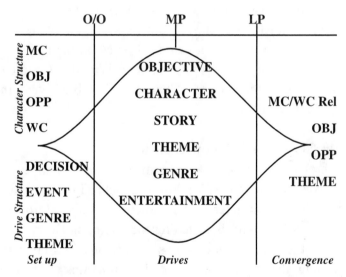

Movies don't just end. They have four resolutions in a genre set piece on the last page. Those resolutions are: The Main Character/Window Character relationship; the Objective; the Opposition; and the Theme.

The resolution of the Character Structure in the third act is what is referred to here as *American Convergence*.

In the diagram above, all elements in the Character Structure as set up in the first act, are resolved in the Convergence. The ideal is to do it on the last page, meaning, in the last scene or sequence.

"Resolution" simply means that we know what happens or what probably will happen. An American movie provides "emotionally satisfying" resolutions. That does not necessarily mean the Main Character gets the Objective, nor does it mean a "happily-ever-after" ending. It means, that whatever happens, it somehow appeals to the audience on an emotional level. A kick in the stomach is OK if it makes sense on an emotional level, if we gain something from the experience. If we're OK with it. Remember, Rocky does not win the fight. Rick does not get Ilsa.

There must be four resolutions in an American Convergence, ideally in a genre set piece on the last page. Those four are: the Main Character/Window Character relationship; the Main Character's Objective; the Opposition; and Theme.

Main Character/Window Character.

Throughout the course of a movie, the audience gets heavily invested in the Window Character. In many ways, the Window Character is the audience's surrogate on the screen; the one who is watching the Main, and very often voicing the audience's opinions, suspicions, and concerns regarding the Main Character. The relationship formed between the Main and Window is a crucial structural element in a well crafted film. The Resolution of this relationship is required or the audience has an empty feeling. Legend has it that when *Casablanca* was in production, the filmmakers did not shoot the last scene of Rick and Louis walking off together. Instinctively they knew something was missing and went back for retakes and added a shot and some lines including "This is the beginning of a beautiful friendship." That is the resolution of the Main Character/Window Character relationship in that movie.

Resolution of Objective.

Resolution of Objective means did the Main Character get the Objective s/he's been pursuing all this time or not? The audience absolutely requires the movie resolve the Main Character's Objective. That does not mean the Main Character *gets* the Objective. It just means that we have to know what happened or will happen.

Resolution of Opposition.

The Opposition Character does not have to die or be defeated. We only need to know what happens. Does he die in a pool of his own blood or does he go on to a greater glory? Does he attain his objective?

In the last scene in *Casablanca*, Victor Laszlo sticks his head up out of nowhere and resolves himself for us: he understands, he forgives, and he is off to save the western world. It's really kind of funny, but to those filmmakers that is what the resolution of Opposition required.

It starts to get dicey when you are using multiple sources of Opposition. Take *Midnight Run* for an example: There are five separate sources of Opposition there and somehow or other they all have to end up in the airport at the end. The FBI, The Mob, Duke, Eddie on the phone, and Marvin, the minion turned Opposition each in their own turn get resolution.

Resolution of Theme.

This is the tricky one. We need to have a sense of what will happen to the Main Character after the FADE OUT. Does he or she get arrested? Die in a pool of his or her own blood? Go on to a greater glory?

The Resolution of Theme answers the question: So what happens to this particular person (MC) who undergoes this particular journey (2nd act), and this particular change?

At the end of *Casablanca*, Rick sends Victor and Ilsa away to safety, kills the Nazi, and walks off with Louis to go help win the war. There were other endings for *Casablanca* offered up. In one, Rick was shot by the Nazi as Victor and Ilsa flew to safety. In another, Rick was arrested and carted off to a concentration camp as Victor and Ilsa flew to safety. In each of those endings the Resolution of Theme is different from the one the film gave the audience.

How would the movie play if one of those alternate endings was used, say where the Nazi shoots Rick instead of the other way around? The resolution of Theme would go like this: A hard-hearted guy like Rick undergoes this journey of the heart to get reconnected with his lost love - and He DIES! THAT'S WHAT HAPPENS! He should have run the minute Ilsa walked in! These women are nothing but trouble! It is easy to see how Resolution of Theme changes the entire movie.

The Resolution of Theme is the biggest place where the writer gets to make his or her particular statement on the human condition. It says to the audience THIS is what happens when you do what the Main just did.

Endings.

The movie is over when the four resolutions occur - *no*

matter what - so the clever writer achieves them all together and ends there, and then writes FADE OUT. If the writer fails to achieve a clear Convergence, the movie goes into anti-climax.

If, for some story-specific reason, the writer cannot achieve the four resolutions together, then they should be ordered from the weakest one (least emotionally satisfying) first, to most powerful one last.

Let's examine the convergence in *Casablanca*, and then see if we can converge that other immortal classic *Og Hunt Kill*.

It is the last scene in *Casablanca* and the entire Character Structure is there: Rick, Ilsa, Victor and Louis. This is Convergence.

Do we resolve the Main Character's Objective (Ilsa)? We certainly do, and in one of the most famous scenes ever written. Rick does not get her, because the problems of three little people don't amount to a hill of beans, etc.

What about the Opposition, (Victor)? Victor sticks his head in between Rick and Ilsa and tells Rick he knows what happened last night, and well, it is okay, he understands. Good old Victor proves noble to the end, and then he's out of there, to save us all from the Nazi scourge. He is resolved.

Do we resolve the Main Character/Window Character relationship? Yes, yes, yes. Rick and Louis go off together with the famous words: "This is the beginning of a beautiful friendship."

Now, the tricky one: Resolution of Theme. What happens to a guy who starts out a cynical, burned out drunk, and ends up the opposite, "Welcome back to the fight, Rick"? Does he "die in a pool of his own blood" or does he "go on to a greater glory"? The screenplay must give us a sense of what comes *after* the FADE OUT. In this movie, the Main Character clearly goes on to greater glory, the message being that doing the noble thing, and the love of good woman, will redeem you forever. If Bogart had been shot or arrested at the end of that movie, as some drafts of the script called for, we would not be talking about *Casablanca* here, fifty some years later.

Og Hunt Kill gets American Convergence.

Onward to our buddy Og and his problems. We will need to resolve the relationship between him and his Neighbor Barney, (Main Character/Window Character). We will want the Opposition, Og's Wife, included in the ending as well. The Objective, Food, somehow plays a part on the last page as well.

Go ahead and set it up. Og is there, the rabbit is his, but he cannot quite bring himself to wack it... but he has to decide. His wife runs in - if the rabbit dies so does their marriage... Neighbor interferes, tries to wack the rabbit but only wounds it... now it's the humane thing to do... Og kills it...

Or,

Og has killed the rabbit in the previous scene, so the Objective has been resolved in advance. He has come back to the cavehouse and offers up dinner to his wife. His wife leaves him. But no, she has second thoughts and comes back. Og rejects her and goes off arm in arm with Barney, the neighbor, to a life of thrilling rabbit killing...

Or,

Og faces the rabbit. The rabbit is quaking in fear. He cannot bring himself to kill it (resolution of Objective). He kills Barney instead, (resolving MC/WC relationship), and tells Wife he loves her and she forgives him, (resolution of Opposition), but drops dead of starvation (resolution of Theme).

Somebody stop me.

Chapter Seven:
THE SEARCH FOR THE SECOND ACT
Creating the Story Line
The Beat and Sequence

Knowing that Character Structure and its accompanying Drive Structure are the essential core elements that make a movie tick, it is possible to understand a movie in only those terms. Stripping a movie down to only these basics leaves out all the wonders that come forth in the actual telling of the story, so, naturally, writers object to their ideas being reduced in this fashion. But writers need to be able to express their movie ideas in only these terms to know for themselves if the ideas *have* these essential core elements and, thus, have a chance to become a good full-length screenplay.

Perhaps the most common mistake new writers make is to have no second act (the "does something" part of Story). Their Main Character does not have a clear Objective in the movie. When new writers tell me how they've been working on a screenplay but can't get past page 30, it's the first symptom of no second act. They started writing without a clear sense of what their Main Character is going to do in the three dimensional world, without a clear Objective, and lo and behold, as soon as they finish the setup, they hit the wall.

Story Line.

The Story Line is a very powerful exercise that puts you

in complete control in the early development stages. It is also a marvelous analytical tool for deconstructing a movie or screenplay to find its problems.

In a basic Story Line, there are three required components: A Main Character with adjective; An Event or Decision; and the Main Character's Objective. These things are then put in a single cause and effect sentence, (usually easiest to begin with the word "when").

Optionally, you can put in the other Structural Characters and Drive components: A Window Character with adjective; An Opposition Character with adjective; more Decisions and/or Events.

The Story line is not intended to be entertaining. Let's take a look at a few different examples of story line and see if you can figure out what's working and what's not working.

```
    When a spacey, but sincere
women goes to the car wash
and discovers that she forgot
her purse, she leaves her
kids there while she goes
home to get it... and never
comes back.
```

Here is the common problem: a movie idea with no second act. The spacey but sincere woman is presented as the Main Character, but she quickly disappears from the movie when she never comes back. This movie actually *begins* when she does not come back. Any writer who attempts to turn this idea into a movie will hit page 20 or 30 and the screenplay will stop dead. But, if you were to say:

> When a spacey, but sincere
> women goes to the car wash
> and discovers that she forgot
> her purse, she leaves her
> kids there while she goes
> home to get it and never
> comes back... so Jose the car
> wash attendant must take the
> kids along on his date to
> Disneyland... (or takes them
> home with him to
> Guatemala...)

Now there's a second act, (or two), and now you have the germ of a movie.

Next example:

> When the most beautiful
> girl in school runs away from
> home, a confident but inexpe-
> rienced boy follows her only
> to get stuck overnight in a
> twenty-four hour truck stop
> where they fall in love with
> each other.

This storyline is describing a Split Main structure. The second act deals with them getting stuck overnight at the truck stop. It's there, but you do not get any sense of what they are actually *doing*. It says they fall in love with each other. Well, we can kind of assume that - after all, there's a Boy, and a Girl, and they're in a movie...

So the second act in this storyline is really only about getting stuck at the truck stop, and it needs to be clearer than that. Add a structural component, say, Opposition. If you say,

```
When the most beautiful
girl in school runs away from
home, a confident but inexpe-
rienced boy follows her only
to get stuck overnight in a
twenty-four hour truck stop
where recruiting the girl
becomes the obsession of
Pauley the pimp who supplies
the truck drivers with hook-
ers.
```

Now there's a better notion of what's going to happen in this movie idea.

Next example:

```
When a booksmart savings
and loan bailout accountant
takes over the business he is
assigned, he discovers it is
a bordello and so he must
confront his conservative
values.
```

Do we have a movie here or not? Well, there's a Main Character with an adjective. He is a booksmart savings and loan bailout accountant. It is a pretty clear definition of who he is. There's an Event, too: he gets assigned a failing business. But what is he doing in the second act? What is his Objective? "He must confront conservative values."

It is assumed he will confront his values in some way. All movies where the Main carries the theme involves self-confrontation. Once you say "booksmart accountant" in the same sentence as "bordello" you've already said he will confront himself. So there's no need to put that into a storyline.

What we need to know is what he actually *does:*

> When a booksmart savings
> and loan bailout accountant
> takes over the business he is
> assigned, he discovers it is
> a bordello and teams up with
> the Madame using his business
> skills to fend off a hostile
> take over and save the busi-
> ness.

Aha. Now you can see a movie emerging.

Next example:

> When a blood thirsty killer
> and his gang are coming to
> kill him, a strong-willed,
> decent cop cannot get any
> help and must fight them
> alone.

Clearly you have a well defined Main Character and a

clear Objective or a second act. This is, of course, *High Noon*. But there is something missing. This Main is a hero so he's still going to be a strong willed, decent cop at the end of the movie. If the writer wanted to include a thematic core in the movie, the story line might read:

```
    When a blood thirsty killer
and his gang are coming to
kill him, a strong-willed,
decent cop must fight them
over the objections of his
pacifist bride who will leave
him if he does.
```

Now the theme starts to show through as the storyline emphasizes what the movie is about on a whole different level.

```
    When a suicidal cop's new
partner takes on a personal
case, the cop must overcome
his self destructiveness long
enough to catch a group of
heroin dealers.
```

So here we have a Main Character/adjective, a clear second act Objective and even a Window Character; this could be a possible story line for *Lethal Weapon*. This is an Action picture with a Main Character on a thematic journey, proving that Character Drive and Story Drive are not mutually exclusive but actually synergistic.

```
    After his car is totalled,
```

an arrogant, young, big-city
doctor meets the woman of his
dreams and must succeed as a
country doctor in order to
win her affection.

This is the Story Line for *Doc Hollywood*. It contains a clear Event, a clearly defined Main Character/adjective and a clear Objective.

Exercise: Referring back to the previous examples and using those examples as a guide, decide for yourself whether the following story ideas have a second act:

When the only woman he has ever
loved, who jilted him some years ago,
walks into his saloon on the arm of
her husband, a cynical American expa-
triate fights to win her back.

When a cynical nightclub owner's long-
lost love shows up in his place, the
old, smoldering feelings are rekindled   *No*
and they struggle to redefine their
relationship.

When a selfish, nasty man's old
girlfriend suddenly and unexpectedly   *No*
shows up, his struggle to win her back
leads to his redemption.

When a man tries to rape one of them
and the other kills him, two suppressed,
intelligent women flee the law.

When he is given a factory full of doomed Jewish workers, a greedy, opportunistic Nazi deceives his taskmasters to save them.

When he finds a lovable alien in his backyard, a bright, trusting, adventuresome eight-year-old boy saves him from the authorities and helps him get back home.

After a tornado carries her off to a strange land, a spunky teenaged girl must face a series of challenges to get home. *vague*

When his blundering uncle throws their building and loan company into insolvency, a despairing small town banker with low self-esteem has to find a way to save the bank.

When a frightened boy moves to a new town with his single mom, he trains with a wise martial arts expert to fight the local bully. *yes*

When his father, the king, is *no* killed, a happy, youthfully exuberant son blames himself and hides out.

The Charting exercise.

If you really want to understand how Character Structure and Drive Structure work in the American Screenplay, do the following at every opportunity you get, on every kind of movie, until it becomes second nature.

Get a video copy of a movie. Sit down with a pad, paper, a pen, a clock, a VCR, and a TV set. Down the left margin of the paper write numbers in multiples of five: 5, 10, 15, 25 and so forth. Start the movie. As the movie unfolds, note on the page what happens at each five-minute mark.

As we have already seen, a movie will run about one page per minute on screen; so if you are thirty minutes into the movie, you are on page thirty of the screenplay. Mark off the Story Structure. What is happening that is significant to the Main Character on page 30? 60? 90? On 45? 75?

Using this book's definitions and guidelines, determine the Character Structure, the Theme, the Event, the Decision, the Drives, all the way through to Convergence.

Watch for the little clues writers drop to provide insight into the Main Character. What is Bogart doing the first time you see him onscreen? (Answer: Playing chess with himself. This is a man at war with himself.) alpha 1 1.

Describe to your satisfaction the "four resolutions in a genre set piece on the last page."

Casablanca is a wonderful movie to start with. It's always nice to know that what we are learning has a long history of success. Pay particularly keen attention to who is sitting around the table at Rick's right around page 30. You will see the entire Character Structure on display and in motion.

Beat and Sequence.

Beat and Sequence are at work on both the story and

scene level. (We'll discuss Beat and Sequence on the scene level in chapter nine, and confine our remarks here to Story.)

A Beat is defined as an Event, Decision, or Discovery that changes the way the Main Character pursues the same Objective.

The spacing of the Beats determines the pacing of the movie. Action pictures have more Beats (and more in the form of Events thus enhancing Story Drive) while Dramas have fewer (and more in the form of Decisions that enhance Character Drive).

After every Beat follows a Sequence, which is a series of scenes that happen as a result. Sequence plays out between Beats. Sequence is to Beat as ripples are to a stone dropped in water.

If the Beats fall at odd intervals, the audience will know something is not right.

A movie can have any amount of Beats. Whatever is not a Beat must be part of a Sequence.

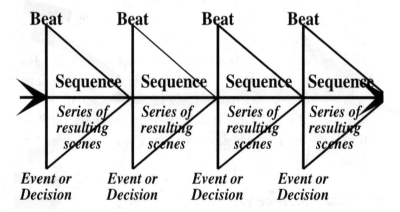

The Beat and Sequence structure is the pacing of the movie

Chapter Eight:
BRINGING IT ALL TOGETHER:
DIAGRAMMING THE MOVIE
The Rack
The Story Diagnostics
The Sag Line

I would like to introduce a visual tool for understanding movies called "The Rack." The Rack is a way of diagramming a movie, just as we used to diagram sentences in fourth grade English. Writing students at The Screenwriters Group in Chicago gave it its name, partly because of what it looks like and partly because it is the rack upon which their movies are often tortured and finally broken apart.

The creative content of a film is of no concern here. This is a diagramming structure. The architect must understand foundations and joists whether s/he is building a barn, skyscraper, or mansion. All people have the same skeleton but not all people look the same. Like everything else, a good screenplay is built from the inside out

Start by drawing out a "time line" for the movie: a horizontal line divided by three equidistant lines into four quarters. Label the three dividing lines with the names O/O, MP, LP. These will correspond to pages 30, 60, and 90, but those page numbers are not critical. The structural passage of the Story is.

Extend vertical lines down from the O/O and LP marks. These lines produce three columns that correspond to the three parts of Story: "A Person" "does something" "it works out."

Next, list the eight required structural elements of the first act set up.

- **The Character Structure.**
    The four structural characters with their adjectives:
    Main Character/adjective
    Objective/adjective
    Opposition/adjective
    Window Character/adjective
Remember the Main's Adjective generates Theme Drive. The Adjectives of all Structural characters in combination *with each other* along with the Objective help generate Entertainment Drive.

    The Objective is optionally a person; it can be anything. Obviously it only gets an Adjective if it is a human being.

- **The Drive Structure.**
    The most common Drive elements (excluding Objective Drive and Entertainment Drive which are in the Character Structure) are then listed separately:
    Decision
    Event
    Genre
    Theme
Theme is also in the Character Structure in the form of the Main Character's Adjective, but it is helpful to list and understand it here, too. It will help us recognize how the journeys of all the Structural Characters play a part in fully developing and expanding Theme Drive.

- **The Journey Markers.**
    Now, across the time line, identify the journey markers. They are O/O, MP, LP.

movie & objective & opposite   *nudge ½ way*   *lost point*

	O/O	MP	LP

Character Structure
MC
OBJ
OPP
WC

Drive Structure
DECISION
EVENT
GENRE
THEME

Set up   *Drives*   *Convergence*

O/O refers to "Objective and Opposition," the moment in the movie when the Main Character has the Objective that is to become The Objective of the movie, and the Opposition is in the movie. The Opposition does not have to be active yet, in Opposition to the Main Character's Objective, just be in the movie.

When those two criteria are met the movie is in the second act. It usually takes around 20 to 30 pages to get that done, but sometimes it happens faster. The point is that no matter what page you are on when that O/O happens, that is when the movie is in its second act.

MP refers to the middle, or MidPoint, of the movie. This appears to be simplistic, but executing it on the page is quite another thing. MidPoint means half way on the Objective quest and/or halfway on the Thematic journey. In better screenplays it's both. What happens at the MidPoint defines page 30 and page 90 with greater authority than anything else. Once you know the MidPoint, you will know the proportions of the entire script. By definition and by logic it is the halfway place, and will occur around page 60 or so.

LP is about Lost Point. The place where, from the perspective of the Main Character, the Objective is no longer attainable. This is what provides the Drive to the Convergence. The Objective is unattainable *unless* the Main takes some drastic action. This will usually take about 90 pages to get to, so page 90 makes for a handy reference, but as in all things in a well-crafted screenplay, it happens where it happens.

Writers need not worry about what page things happen on. In a well-crafted screenplay, everything hits the page numbers as diagrammed here without being forced. Page count is a by product of proper structure, not the goal of proper structure.

	O/O	MP	LP	
Character Structure MC				
OBJ		OBJECTIVE		
OPP		CHARACTER		
WC		STORY		
		THEME		
Drive Structure DECISION		GENRE		
EVENT		ENTERTAINMENT		
GENRE				
THEME				
	Set up	*Drives*	*Convergence*	

• **Convergence.**

Next, in the right hand column, put down the four resolutions that must occur.

> Main Character/Window Character relationship.
> Opposition.
> Objective.
> Theme.

Note the four resolutions are the same as the Character
Structure from the first act. A movie is an organic singular-
ity and that's it. It starts and ends with the same people. In
Figure 4 the Rack is drawn to include which Drive elements
create what and a double ellipse to represent the beginning
middle and convergence of the Character Structure.

This diagram is particularly handy for "deconstructing"
a movie or finished script. If you are starting a new screenplay, do not expect to understand your piece in this depth

	O/O	MP	LP
Character Structure **MC**			
OBJ		**OBJECTIVE**	
OPP		**CHARACTER**	**MC/WC Rel**
WC		**STORY**	**OBJ**
		THEME	**OPP**
Drive Structure **DECISION**		**GENRE**	
EVENT		**ENTERTAINMENT**	**THEME**
GENRE			
THEME			
	Set up	*Drives*	*Convergence*

Everything in a movie determines everything else.

right away. Use it as guide to continually prompt and guide your developmental thinking, and not as a challenge to be answered in a definitive way once and for all on the first day of writing.

Keeping with everyone's favorite movie example as developed in previous chapters, we will put *Casablanca* on the The Rack first, and then do the same for our contribution to cinema history, *Og Hunt Kill.*

Character Structure on the Rack.
In the left hand column is a list that begins with Main Character (MC) on top. I do not think there is much argument in that Rick is the Main Character in *Casablanca.*

The second question is: if Rick is the Main Character, what is his Objective? Rick has shown no interest in anything up to this point, and then SHE walks in right around page 30. Put down Ilsa's as Objective.

Who is the Opposition? If Rick's Objective is Ilsa, why can't he have her? She's married. Victor, then, is the Opposition.

Who is the Window Character? Who is the person through whom we see the changes in the Main Character? The one to whom the Main Character speaks the most, the one who is there from beginning to end and at every critical moment of the Main Character's life? And the one who says things like, "Oh, Rick, you've never done this before." Yes, it is Captain Renault. The classic Window Character.

The Thematic Adjective(s). How would you describe the Main Character in in the beginning of the movie? Rick is a cynic, he's a burn out, he's a drunkard, he's tough, he's cool, he's dropped out of life, all of these things. He's a loner. He sticks his neck out for nobody, which is some-

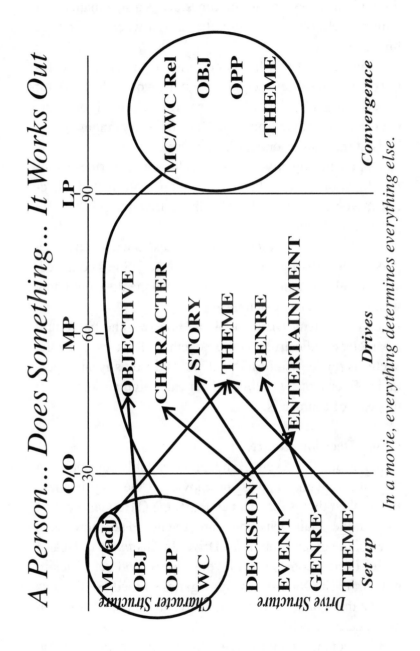

A Person... Does Something... It Works Out

thing he says about a million times. He is also a man at war with himself, playing chess with himself when we first see him onscreen.

Compare that to who he becomes at the end. He commits the great selfless act, giving up the woman he loves for the greater good. The little changes Rick shows through the course of the movie from who he is in the beginning to who he is at the end generates Theme Drive.

Opponent adjective. How would you describe Victor Laszlo in outwardly directed, relationship-oriented adjectives? Noble, pure, wealthy, brilliant, driven to succeed. He is all these things.

The Objective's adjective. In this case the Objective is a person: Ilsa. How would you describe her? She's confused, she's loyal, she's in love with two men, she does not know where her allegiance belongs.

Entertainment Drive: look at how all the Structural Characters' adjectives come together. Rick is a cynic. Victor is noble. Ilsa is ambivalent. And Louis is an opportunist. Even a bad writer could get entertainment snap from this cast of characters.

Event, Decision, Genre.

What are the Events, and, most notably, the one big Causal Event that makes the movie go the way it goes? Remember, things that happen that are NOT under the control of the Main Character are Events. The more such Events, the greater the Story Drive. In *Casablanca*, Ugarte (Peter Lorre), comes in with "the papers" and begs Rick to hide him. The Nazis show up. Ugarte is killed. SHE walks in. By this point, with all these Events, Story Drive is in high gear.

Decision. Character Drive runs on things happening that

ARE under the control of the Main Character. You want to write your movie in such a way that the Main Character is presented with direct Yes or No decisions or with having to do something they just said or showed us they wouldn't do in a million years.

First, Ugarte runs into the club: "Rick, Rick help me, hide me..." Rick refuses. That's a Decision. But, as we see, a "No" does not make for a Decision that Drives.

Then, "Will you take these papers??" Now Rick faces another decision. He Decides, Yes, he will take these papers -- a very clear Decision. And, better yet, a yes.

Decision is further compounded by the actions Rick takes after Ilsa enters the movie. He chooses to make a whole series of Decisions that increase the power of the movie's Character Drive.

Genre Set Piece: what is the genre of the movie? It is a Romance, a bit Noir, perhaps. Can we see it throughout the film? Is it on the first page and the last? Certainly the last page is crying with Romance and the appropriate visual style.

The Journey Markers and the Drives.

The Main Character Objective is Ilsa. She walks in not just with a husband, but a husband-hero, the perfect, built-in Opposition to Rick, and they, together with Window Character Louis, all come together just before page 30. So, in the case of *Casablanca*, the O/O, or second act start, is just before page 30.

MP means Mid Point. The screenplay is halfway through. Is the Main Character halfway through his/her journey? How do we know? We need an indication, in the form of action, that the Main Character is making progress toward his future self.

When Rick helps the Romanian couple win some money to get out -- a selfless mini-act, Rick's first -- that's the thematic MidPoint.

The Story MidPoint is: there is only one way out of Casablanca and that is through Rick.

There are a number of different ways to execute a Mid Point. It can be a loss of options; the first confrontation between the Main Character and the Opposition; or a change of Objective. It's OK to be creative. Just understand that once the writer commits to the MidPoint, then story at 30 and 90 becomes evident, downright inevitable.

At the three quarters mark you find the LP, which means Lost Point. Here, the Objective is lost from the Main Character's point of view, unless s/he takes overt action to change the course of events. What happens at the LP "Casablanca"? Ilsa points a gun at Rick, and Rick says: "Go ahead and shoot. You'd be doing me a favor." Rick knows he will never get Ilsa.

Four Resolutions.

The Main Character/Window Character Relationship must be resolved. Do Rick and Louis resolve their relationship? They not only resolve it, but they do it in the most famous movie line ever written: "This is the beginning of a beautiful friendship."

Objective. Remember, resolving the Objective does not mean the Main Character *gets* the Objective. It means we know what happens and we're OK with it. In this case Rick wants Ilsa. Is it resolved? Yes. Does he get her? No.

Opposition. The question is not whether the Opposition wins or loses, but what happens to him. Take another look at the last scene. Out of nowhere, Victor sticks his head into the scene between Rick and Ilsa, has some dialog where he says he knows what happened between them and that all is forgiven and off he goes. Yes, the Opposition is resolved.

Theme. Resolution of Theme gives us a sense of what is *going to* happen to the Main Character after the FADE OUT. Rick goes off to a greater glory. So, what happens to a drunken, burned out, cynic who is somehow able to redeem himself through the love of a woman? He has a chance to attain a greater glory in life.

Resolution of Theme is where the writer gets a chance to make the big statement on the Human Condition. A screen-play is pretty much determined by the Characters, but the Resolution of Theme can be chosen by the writer.

Genre Set Piece. Was that a genre set piece at the end? Was it Romantic, standing on the tarmac in the fog with the plane turning its propellers behind them? Call me mushy, but I think it was. It was moody and dark and foggy and she looked beautiful and the two of them were in love and wearing hats.

A Person... Does Something... It Works Out

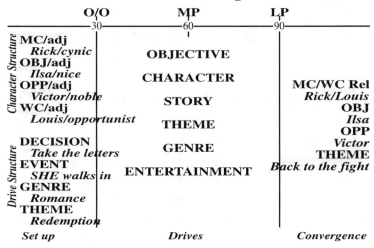

	O/O	MP	LP
	—30—	—60—	—90—
Character Structure **MC/adj** *Rick/cynic* **OBJ/adj** *Ilsa/nice* **OPP/adj** *Victor/noble* **WC/adj** *Louis/opportunist*		**OBJECTIVE** **CHARACTER** **STORY** **THEME**	**MC/WC Rel** *Rick/Louis* **OBJ** *Ilsa* **OPP** *Victor*
Drive Structure **DECISION** *Take the letters* **EVENT** *SHE walks in* **GENRE** *Romance* **THEME** *Redemption*		**GENRE** **ENTERTAINMENT**	**THEME** *Back to the fight*
	Set up	*Drives*	*Convergence*

Casablanca on the The Rack.

Did the four resolutions in a genre set piece occur on the last page? Absolutely. FADE OUT, the end.

This may seem confusing at first. Then again, writing a 120-page screenplay is not simple. For those of you who want to write one, the Rack is a powerful tool.

> *Applying the Rack to an existing screenplay or movie quickly reveals what's working, what's not working, and why.*

Remember, all of movie structure depends on the length of the finished script. If you know it is going to be a hundred and twenty pages long, you know before you write one word that page sixty is going to be half way, and so forth. You know you are going to want Story Drive, Character Drive, Genre, Entertainment, and Theme Drive, and the Rack will give you the tools to get those Drives running and to control their relative strength.

"OG HUNT KILL" GOES ON THE RACK

We should now be able to put the elements of "Og Hunt Kill" on the Rack without any trouble provided, of course, that we have developed it into an American Movie.

Character Structure:

Main Character (first person to make a decision), is *Og*; Objective (what he will come to want in the beginning), is *Food*; Opposition (the obstacle in his way) is his *Wife*; Window Character (the one he talks to) is his *Neighbor, Barney*.

Drive Structure:

Event(s), (something that occurs that is outside the control of the Main Character), are, *Meteorite falls, loss of food supply.*

Decision(s) (something that occurs that IS under the control of the Main Character) is *Hunt.*

Thematic adjectives (words that describe the person in a social context--NOT job titles or a resume, NOT praise of the person's deeds, NOT internal issues, NOT introspective qualities, NOT inactive attributes), are *Vegetarian/Pacifist.*

Applying adjectives to the rest of the character structure (remember the adjectives should be complementary in order to heighten entertainment value), we would probably say Og's wife can be either super militant vegetarian or super pacifist. Let's go with pacifist. Let's make the neighbor the super militant hunter, president of the National Spear Association.

Genre (what *kind* of movie is it). We will decide right up front to make our movie, *Og Hunt Kill*, an Action/Adventure film.

For reference, the "Og Hunt Kill" story line was:

```
When a meteor comes to earth and wipes
out his food source, a vegetarian paci-
fist cave man must hunt over the objec-
tion of his pacifist wife.
```

Let's go through The Rack a couple more times for practice. You do not need to screen the following films to understand the exercise. It will become self-explanatory as you proceed.

Lets' do the Rack for *Thelma and Louise* and *Midnight*

Run. These two movies are already "old" movies as of this writing. These are movies that people remember because of their content, not because of their ad budgets.

These two movies also use different applications of Character Structure and will give us an opportunity to examine specific applications of split mains and multiple opposition.

Thelma and Louise

Character Structure

Who is the Main Character: Who's the person who makes the first decisions in the movie, or makes the big Decision(s) that determine the course of the movie?

Both Thelma and Louise fit those definitions, and as it is possible to split and combine any of the components in the Character Structure to suit your story, Thelma and Louise, by definition, are both Main Characters. The script has a **split main** structure.

Split mains are usually each other's Window Character. The main reason for this is that you have limited space in a screenplay. Both Mains can have other friends that they talk to, but the easiest way to create a Window Character who will be in the movie at the beginning and end is to make each Main the other's Window.

Now, what sort of adjectives shall we attach to our Mains? Clearly, one is oppressed and one is a free spirit. Thelma wants some measure of freedom and respect from her husband. Louise wants her boyfriend to commit to their relationship. But they are both trying to gain control of their lives.

We are getting a notion of who they are in the beginning. They are different, but similarly motivated. They perfectly complement each other.

What do they want? What are the two Objectives (one for each Main Character) in the first quarter of the movie? At first they want to leave their men for a weekend in order to get the men to behave in a certain way, but soon they are fleeing for their lives. In a split main construction, the Objectives should be different but closely related.

Who is the Opposition? Who is standing in their way? The cop (Harvey Keitel). Again, the opponent is the nicest guy in the world. He has their best interests at heart. He is trying to bring them in so they do not get hurt.

Decision

Remember, Decision is defined as things that happen under the control of the Main Character. The more Decisions a Main Character makes, the stronger the Character Drive. In most movies, one decision made near the beginning of the movie stands above the rest. Call this one the Fateful Decision.

Thelma and Louise features a number of important Decisions made by both characters. Should I take the gun? Should we stop for a drink? Should I dance with that cowboy? The result is an extremely strong Character Drive. The audience is behind Thelma and Louise because we see them make these decisions, but the Fateful Decision(s) is to kill the cowboy and flee.

Added snap is attained in Character Drive when characters make Decisions that run contrary to what we know to be that character's nature. This will always enhance the impact of character drive. When an oppressed housewife goes off without telling her oppressing husband, when she kicks up her heels, she gets the audience's attention.

Event

Event is something(s) that happens that is not under the control of the Main Character. The Event of this movie is the cowboy's attempted rape of Thelma.

Genre

Action-Road-Buddy. Genre set piece: car chase.

To sum up the first act setup: Thelma and Louise are a split main acting as each other's Window Character. Their Objective is to get to Mexico, and the Opposition is the cop. The Event is the rape. The Decisions are many, making this clearly a character-driven, action movie.

Convergence

Was the Main Character/Window Character relationship resolved? Yes. The two Mains, each other's Windows, went off the cliff together in the car holding each other's hand in a statement of solidarity and love.

Resolution of Objective: their Objective was to escape. Well, yes and no, but they achieved it, one way or another. So it was resolved.

Was the Opposition resolved? Yes again, despite real-life obstacles to the resolution. Harvey Keitel was brought into the last scene even though he had no jurisdiction there, no business being there, and though many did not want him there. He had to be there, the only one running after the car as it headed for the cliff, because he is the Opposition.

Did we resolve the Theme? Remember, the resolution of theme gives us a sense of what happens to a person who undergoes this journey after the FADE OUT. What happens to two women who are reaching out to gain some control in their lives? What happens to them when they reach out for freedom? Well, in this case they die for their trouble. This movie took a lot of criticism for its ending. To some it appeared to be saying: "Well, *girls,* this is what happens to you if you reach for freedom." Resolution of Theme defines the movie in powerful ways. Would it have been as powerful if they had lived and gotten away?

Was the movie resolved in a genre set piece? Action picture = car chase. Yes.

Finally, did all four resolutions occur on the last page or in one final, cohesive sequence? Yes.

Story Structure

A movie is in its second act when the Main Character has an Objective and the Opponent is in the picture. This movie enters its second act when Harvey Keitel appears.

MidPoint is half way through the journey. There are a number of ways of executing a mid point. It is often done when something previously unknown about the character becomes known; when a certain major subtext becomes text. Often the Main Character will meet or recognize the Opponent at the MidPoint. Sometimes an event will occur which limits the Main Character's options to only one, thereby putting the movie on a collision course to convergence. Often an Objective changes at the MidPoint.

What happens halfway through *Thelma and Louise*? The money is stolen, taking away all but one of the women's options. Later, Harvey Keitel actually tells Brad Pitt: "When you took that money you took away all their options."

The theft has the exact effect of putting the movie on a collision course to Convergence. Up to this point the two women had a lot of options open to them, but after that point there is only one.

Lost Point

The point at which the Objective is no longer attainable from the Main Character's perspective. Thelma and Louise realize they cannot go home; the police have gained complete control of their environment; and they realize they don't want to go home. They are caught, hopeless... UNLESS...

That completes the Rack for *Thelma and Louise*. Once you have done the exercise, the easiest way to understand the movie is to diagram its components on the Rack.

The second example is *Midnight Run* with Robert DeNiro and Charles Grodin. It is another buddy-action-road-except-with-comedy picture, but it does something different with Character Structure. I'll use this as an example to compare and contrast two similar movies to show what changes in Character Structure will do.

Main Character

Right off we can see that Jack is a tough, cynical, smart, burned out, ex-cop, but most of all, honest. In fact, Jack is irrationally honest, painfully honest. He is going to do what he feels is right even if it means wasting in poverty. He'll turn down a million dollars to keep his agreement for $100,000. He is a complex individual, though, and he will steal a car if it serves his purpose. He is honest to his own code of honesty.

Objective

Dream Objective: Open a coffee shop. Movie Objective: Get the Duke to L.A. on time.

Opposition

Can there be more than one Opponent in a movie? Yes. Everyone seems to be after the Duke, so everyone seems to have an Objective that excludes Jack's. One must be careful here not to confuse Opponent with Minion. If the Main is opposed by someone who is working for the Opponent, structurally it is still just one source of opposition. If two characters are working on their own Objectives, and those objectives run against the Main Character's Objective, then those two become separate sources of opposition, and that puts multiple Opposition Characters in the Rack.

For example, when Dorothy killed the Wicked Witch, the flying monkeys were no longer a threat to her. The Witch was the Opponent and the monkeys her minions. In *Romancing the Stone*, the Minister of Antiquities and Danny DeVito were both after the stone for their own purposes, providing two separate sources of opposition for the Main. Unlike the monkey minions, if you take one out, you still have the other to deal with.

Midnight Run develops a ton of Opponents. There's the Mob Boss, the FBI agent, the Bailbondsman, the minion-turned-opposition Marvin, and the Duke himself. The mobster, Jimmy Serrano, has his two thugs ("moron number one and moron number two") operating as minions. The FBI is personified in Alonzo Moseley and the hundreds of feds and cops who come after the Duke are listed in his minion column.

There's more. There is Marvin Dorfler, the other bounty hunter. But is he a source? Eddie Moscone, the bailbondsman sends Marvin after Jack and Duke. So Eddie would be the source of Opposition and Marvin his minion. But once Marvin knows what's going down he comes after the Duke on his own - Eddie isn't the only one willing to pay for the

Duke. And in fact, he tries to sell the Duke to the mob entirely on his own. So maybe we could promote Marvin from minion to Opposition in his own right at the point where he starts working for himself.

Perhaps the most significant Opponent in all this is the Duke himself. He clearly has an Objective that runs contrary to the Mains: he wants to get away. Duke does everything he can to stop Jack from achieving his Objective because it means curtains for Duke if he does.

As we have seen, it is possible to split and combine structural characters. *Midnight Run* has four separate sources of Opposition. That means every time Jack and Duke turn around some opponent or minion is jumping out at them. The effect is to increase the pace of the movie.

Window Character

To whom does Jack talk? Through whom do we see what's going on in Jack's head? Clearly, it is the Duke who's Jack's Window Character. He's there, essentially, through the entire movie. He's there for the denouement. He's the person to whom Jack bares his soul.

Summing up the Character Structure: Main Character Jack (Robert DeNiro), the last honest man in the world, takes on the Objective of getting Duke (Charles Grodin) to L.A. on time. Besides Duke himself, he battles three separate sources of Opposition: the mob (Jimmy Serrano), the FBI (Alonzo Moseley), and the bailbondsman (Eddie Moscone), while revealing himself to Window Character Duke.

Event

As usual, there are a lot of Events, that is, things that happen that are not under the control of the Main Character, and then there is the one central causal Event that starts the movie in motion: Jack is offered the job. The Events start to pile up quickly in this script - the more Events the greater the value of the Story Drive.

Decision

As opposed to Event, Decisions are things that happen that *are* under the control of the Main Character. There are a lot of Decisions in this movie, but the big one, the "Fateful Decision" is to take the job. All the little things he does all along way also constitute Decisions. The more Decisions, the greater the Character Drive.

Convergence

Does *Midnight Run* end in the four resolutions of the classic American convergence?

Does it: Resolve the Main Character/Window Character relationship? Jack and Duke are at the phone booth. Jack calls Moscone and tells him he is freeing the Duke because Moscone lied to him. He hangs up, gives the Duke his wrist watch and walks away. The Duke calls him back and gives him a money belt containing three hundred thousand dollars, adding their catch line, "See you in the next life." Off Jack goes to open his coffee shop and off goes the Duke in the other direction. So, yes, we resolve the relationship between the Main Character and the Window Character.

Does it: Resolve the Opposition, or, in this case, five separate sources of Opposition? At the airport, somehow they are all there for the big show down. The F.B.I. (Moseley) gets his man (Serrano) and lets Jack go. The mobster gets busted and therefore does not get Duke. Moscone could not make it to the airport, so we see him instead talking on the phone to his henchmen at the airport and then with Jack for the big kiss off. Duke leaves on his own. And, of course, the hapless Marvin wanders into it all and gets busted.

All of the opposition and all of their minions were thrown into the mix at the end in a single, grand Convergence.

Does it: Resolve the Objective, which was to get Duke to L.A. on time? Yes, we resolved it. He would have made it, but is able to let the Duke go. But what about the "dream objective," the coffee shop. That, too, is resolved by implication.

Resolution does not mean success. It means that the audience knows what happened or will happen, and accepts it.

Did the movie resolve the Theme? Resolution of Theme means the script gives us a sense of what will happen to the Main Character after the FADE OUT. So, what happens to a Main Character who is a painfully honest man, who goes through this particular journey and comes to the end in this way. Does he end up dead in a pool of his own blood? Does he go to prison? Does he ends up a pauper? Or, does he walk off into the L.A. night with three hundred thousand dollars tucked in his pocket?

Imagine the effect instead if he had turned around, given the Duke his watch, said "See you in the next life," and walked out the door into the rainy night penniless. You would have had an entirely different movie, and probably not a comedy-action.

Story Structure

The Second Act begins when the Main Character has an Objective and the Opposition, or in this case all of the Opposition, is in the movie.

This happens immediately in *Midnight Run*. Jack gets his Objective (right after the obligatory "action opener") and then immediately meets all of the Opposition people. By the time Moscone/Dorfler, Serrano/morons, and Moseley/FBI are in, the movie is in its Second Act. This happens pretty quickly here.

The MidPoint. Jack goes from saying, "I do not care what is right or wrong, I am going to do what I said I was going to do," to the end of the movie where he finally finds a way to bend a little and free the Duke. What is halfway along his journey?

Halfway in the story of a cross-country trip would obviously be arriving someplace like Chicago. Halfway on the Thematic Journey has big tough Jack softening. It's when they visit Jack's ex-wife in Chicago, when Jack calls Duke "John" for the first time, and when Jack's daughter comes out and Jack quietly goes to pieces when he sees her.

Story MidPoint might be in the next sequence, when Jack realizes that Eddie's phone is tapped and knows that the chase is really on now.

Lost Point

The point at which the Main's Objective is lost would clearly be when Jack is arrested. He is going to prison. He is facing a pile of charges. Moseley is going to be there to walk him into the prison. All is lost *unless* he takes a strong, compelling action to alter events.

Jack comes up with the idea to swap the discs for the Duke, and the game is on again. The "it works out," or third act, of the movie is now driven into motion by a Decision completely consistent with who the Main is and what his Objective is.

Convergence

Four resolutions occurred in a genre set piece on the last page, despite the multiple sources of Opposition in the movie.

Did it converge in a genre set piece? The movie was comedy-action-buddies all the way through. It was all genre set pieces. Never let you down.

Chapter Nine:
SCENE
The three functions of scene
Cinematic Narrative
The three kinds of scene
The four page elements of scene
Scene diagnostics
The Scene Rack
Shaping the page
Dialog

Two distinct, unrelated styles of writing go into a screenplay: Story and Scene. No training is transferrable from one to the next.

DON'T

I encourage you not to start your scene work until you have written your story out from start to finish in plain prose. You don't want to be trying to find your way through the story while writing scenes. When you write out your story (whether you call it a treatment, an outline, or a synopsis), USE NO DIALOG. Dialog is for scenes only. Make sure all your structural components are in place before you write one word of the first scene.

When it comes to writing a scene you have to forget all about story.

Scene takes place in the moment and nowhere else. The characters in your scenes are people and, like real people, the characters in the scene do not know where their life story is going. They can only live in the present moment.

Now, please get this straight:

> *The primary function of scene and dialog is NOT to push your story forward.*

The forward momentum of story is a byproduct of properly chosen, constructed, and assembled scenes. The story movement comes through between the scenes. The scene itself does not tell any story. Each scene has its own integrity within its own moment. A scene deals with what is happening right here, right now, between the people on the screen.

The Three Functions of Scene:
Technical, Narrative, and Moment

The *production-related* function of a scene is the *Technical* function; it is what the writer puts in for the people who must actually make the picture.

Scenes have another function in the way they attach to one another. This is how the Story is told and I will call it the *Narrative* function of scene.

There is the *dramatic* function of scene, the here and now of the movie; I will call it *Moment*.

The technical function

The writer has to tell all the craft people, from the director to the production assistants, what s/he wants in a scene. Essential information includes: the set or location where the scene takes place; the time of day, for lighting purposes; props required; and cast members in the scene.

Everyone who works in movies reads the screenplay primarily to get what they want from it. They all want vastly different things, and it is your job to write for all of them. Your scene is going to be used for very specific technical purposes.

Clarity in the technical calls will also result in an accurate budget. The Unit Production Manager or Assistant Director needs to know a lot of specific, technical things about the movie. How many sets are needed, how many are on stage interiors, how many on location, the kind of lighting package required, and so forth. Clarity in your work will result in an accurate budget and schedule. I'm not saying you should write to any given budget, I'm saying you should write clearly in terms of the technical needs. Producers frequently will go looking for scripts with a budget in mind. If your technical information is not clear, the budget person is going to estimate high for safety.

A common error in this technical area is made in sluglines. If you call for a scene in the study, say,

```
INT    STUDY    NIGHT
```

on page ten, and later on page twenty it's,

```
INT    DEN    NIGHT
```

which to the writer is obviously the same room, it's not to the budgeter, who will call for two sets-at double the cost. I'm not saying write cheap, I'm saying be accurate and consistent.

General technical guidelines: Always use either DAY or NIGHT on every slug unless it's essential to the story that you use DAWN, or a specific time of day, but even then the

don't use

writer can expect to see either day or night on the screen. If you feel it absolutely necessary to use CONTINUOUS in your slug, put it after DAY or NIGHT. Be kind to your budget, schedule, and lighting people.

Don't specify things such as make, model and year of an automobile, the names of the music playing or the book a character is reading unless it is imperative to the story. Endless, superfluous detail and description will only hurt you rather than help you.

Write so that anyone can understand what you're trying to say. Use words as structural armatures, not as decorative filigree.

The narrative function

This is the story telling part. No, a scene does not tell the story. The story is told in how the scenes attach one to the next. Narrative is created from the way you put scenes together. This is interpreted in the minds of the audience as a continuous event even though the scenes are not actually continuous. This creation of story in the minds of the audience happens quite independently of the content of the scene.

For instance. Here's a story told in three scenes:

```
1. A woman gambles wildly at a crap
table in a posh casino. She's having a
grand old time, the money is flying.

                              CUT TO

2. A car drives madly across the
desert at night.
```

                                        CUT TO

    3. The woman at the bedside of her
dying mom, who, with a kind and knowing smile, dies.

    Now, let's do a little shake and bake. Same three scenes:

    1. The woman at the bedside of her
dying mom, who, with a kind and knowing smile, dies.

                                        CUT TO

    2. A car drives madly across the
desert at night.

                                        CUT TO

    3. A woman gambles wildly at a crap
table in a posh casino. She's having a
grand old time, the money is flying.

    By messing with the way the scenes attach one to the
other, an entirely different narrative, or story, emerges. This
has nothing to do with the scenes themselves. The function
inside the scene is NOT to push the story this way or that,
but to pursue needs, as the character feels them at that place
and time.
    This is where a lot of writers go to pieces. It is confusing to
say, on the one hand, that scenes do not push the story, and
then, on the other hand, point out the narrative function of
scenes. This is what gave rise to the 3x5 index card method

of trying to make a story out of individual scenes written on cards and then mixed and matched into different scenarios.

On the shot level: Take a shot of a train coming down the tracks. Then, take a shot of a guy in a black suit tying a woman to the tracks. Then, take a shot of a guy galloping on a white horse, and cut them together. In the minds of the audience, that train is on the same tracks that guy is tying the girl to. And that guy on the white horse is galloping toward the same place. In fact, even though it's not on the screen, the audience will insist that all three events, the villain, the train, and the hero, are about to converge.

When you put scenes together, you are going to be telling a story. The audience is going to see a story. In fact, the audience makes up the story, and the clever writer teases Story out of the audience through cinematic narrative. Stringing together scenes, like pearls on a necklace, will evoke an overall impression in the mind of the audience that is not necessarily ever on the screen.

So, what is it? How does it work? Where does it come from? Cinematic narrative is really what we deal in when we try to tell stories on film. And scene is our *only* tool.

When film began, it was a sensation because it was perceived as a still picture that moved. People would go into a nickelodeon and would see actors pantomiming something. There were no edits. They would come out dazed by the reality of what they saw. There was a tremendous excitement about it. It was a moving picture. Silent, but nonetheless a powerful, state-of-the-art media experience.

Around the year 1903, Edwin Porter came along and wondered what would happen if he took a moving picture of something over there and a moving picture of something over here and back over there and cut them all together. To his delight, even though the pictures weren't related to each other, that is, not shot in the same time or place, the audience related them in time and space and, not only that, the audience went on to invent what was happening in between. In between the stuff they did see, the audience was able to tell you what was going on in the world of that movie. They invented a whole story to go along with the pictures they were seeing.

This is cinematic narrative. The narrative is brought in by the audience. Don't ever get the notion that you are leading the audience along. "Oh Great Writer" is going to take the audience some place where they have never been. That's not going to happen. The audience comes in with stories already built into their brains. They have all seen movies before. They know what a movie is and should be. They are coming to your movie only to gain new perspectives and insights into their existing notions. So the narrative comes into the theatre on the minds of the audience. The audience has expectations. They come with a momentum, and your job is to stay out of the way, and if you're lucky, slightly ahead of them. You are not so much leading them as trying not to get trampled by them.

The narrative function of the cinema is the uniqueness of what screenwriters do. We are able to transport an audience through time and space on a grander scale than any medium that has ever come before. Your strength as a screenwriter is to be able to spin a narrative by flying through time and space and people effortlessly. That's what has to happen when you are putting your scenes together.

The point is that your movie is an organic whole. What comes before profoundly effects what comes after, and vice versa. Understand that scenes are like brush strokes on a painting. You cannot put a red streak on the Mona Lisa and say it's just one stroke and it doesn't affect the whole painting. Yes, it does. Especially when the audience knows there is no red streak on Mona.

The moment function

The function of moment is the *here and now* of the movie: the moment-to-moment of what the audience is, and the characters are, feeling.

Moment comes off the screen according to the needs of the people in the scene: how badly they need what they need; how they choose to pursue those needs from the people around them, right here and now, on the screen. "Moment" in this context means: What is the audience feeling NOW? Each moment, moment to moment. This is why there should be no scenes in a movie that build up to anything or are waiting for something to happen. All scenes where people talk must be raised to 100% of the possible urgency, given the situation, at all times, in order to satisfy the requirement of Moment.

Any scene where people talk is a dramatic scene. The function of the dramatic scene is to invest the movie with the vital "here and now," or *moment*, upon whose altar the writer and movie will live or die.

Three kinds of scenes:
Mechanic, Kinetic and Dramatic

Sometimes a scene simply moves people around for the needs of the narrative. The Character crosses the street, takes a plane, etc. Call that *Mechanics*.

There are scenes and sequences that add a lot of flash and dazzle to a movie, but do not move people around or pit needs in opposition, and simply hope to increase the entertainment value of the movie. We will call these *Kinetic*.

Then there are ~~are~~ the scenes where ③ people talk. People only talk in a movie when they want something from the person they're talking to. We will call those scenes *Dramatic.*③

Mechanic

Mechanical scenes can help smooth the narrative flow, but they do not convey dramatics, or people speaking. These would include ESTABLISHING shots and transitional scenes.

If the character travels from place to place in the story, it is sometimes useful to include a sequence showing a jet taking off, or a bus pulling up, the exterior of the character's home, so we know how and where we're going. Usually, though, the audience will get it if the movie just cuts from one place to the other.

I had a writer ask me once: "The characters are in the Middle East and I have to get them to Chicago. How do I do it?" The answer is: CUT TO -

```
EXT   O'HARE AIRPORT - DAY
```

The audience will fill in all the rest.

Use Mechanical scenes carefully. They will more often bog down the narrative flow than help it out. It may be the writer's first time in the theatre, but the audience has been here many times before and they are extremely fast in putting the pieces together.

Kinetics

A scene that does not relocate anything, does not smooth out the narrative flow, does not put anyone in conflict, but sparkles at us from the screen is purely kinetic. These are popular with some directors and are more in their realm than the writers'. For an example of Kinetics, screen the first half of *Natural Born Killers*.

Dramatics.

The primary function of scenes is not to push your story forward. While we're in the negative mode of expression, here are some more things that scenes do NOT do:

NO expository scenes in a screenplay,
NO scenes for mood, tone, color,
NO scenes to "show" anything,
NO scenes to "tell" anything,
NO scenes that build up to something,
NO scenes that drop down from anything,
NO scenes to give information or backstory,

...EXCEPT AS A BYPRODUCT OF CONFLICT!

Conflict does not mean "fight." It does not mean go for the guns. It means: *Needs in Opposition.*

When we were kids we were taught that a story has ups and downs like a roller coaster. Some well-meaning teacher plotted a jagged line on a graph representing time elapsed on one axis and dramatic value on the other. Maybe it was right for your fourth grade class on composition, but now I am telling you to forget that. A movie does not go up and down. It goes straight ahead, straight across.

Writers and analysts of screenplays must understand the nature of *one hundred percent intensity* in a movie. It has to do with the concept of "moment."

I'm telling you now, writer to writer, that when you are faced with a blank page, all these notions of a movie going up and down will only defeat you. You must approach each blank page as a challenge to find the one hundred per cent intense interaction possible given the characters and their needs in that moment, right here, right now.

One hundred percent intensity means the Main Character is totally involved in each and every moment on screen. That does not mean that every moment in the Main Character's life is equally memorable. It means that the action and the characters are always at one hundred percent *in each moment*, from *moment to moment* in a movie. The moment is all-important.

Let's say you owe me money and I am going to get it from you no matter what. We're standing out on a street corner and I'm saying: "Gimme my money or else!" I'm really intense and the veins are standing out on my neck and I am at one hundred percent intensity. What I don't know is that around the corner there is a Tyrannosaurus Rex that is about to step up and give one hundred percent intensity an entirely new meaning. But that doesn't mean I *wasn't* at one hundred percent in the moment before.

In the first Moment, arguing for money, I don't know what is about to come around the corner. The second Moment may be a stronger one hundred percent relative to the previous moment, but it was still one hundred percent *in both Moments,* given the possibilities of the situation.

Think of a movie as a straight line from start to finish, and that line represents one hundred percent intensity. The nature of one hundred percent means one hundred percent in the character's mind, *at that moment* and *in that place,* without regard to what will be happening later in the movie.

Scenes can be for entertainment only

Not all scenes move the story. Sometimes people can talk to each other in a scene and it is purely entertaining.

Characters sitting around a table telling jokes in a movie is not necessarily dramatic or overtly dealing with needs in opposition, but if it's funny and memorable it might work in context, especially with a strong subtext. (i.e. *Good Will Hunting*.)

The structure of scene

So, what happens in the moment? What makes a good scene? All successful dramatic scenes have certain elements in common.

Drama

The Dramatic Scene presents *needs in opposition*: someone wants something from another person and the other person wants something from him, *in this moment in this place.*

As a writer, you need to organize your thinking in terms of moment-to-moment needs. When two (or more) people want something from each other that they cannot have, right here and right now, you have *drama*.

To create the dramatic scene you must know the following:

> *What does character A want from character B that he can't have; What does character B want from character A that she can't have - Right here - Right now.*

If you do not know the answer to this question, do not write the scene. Writers who start a scene without identifying the needs in opposition first, end up going on and on, page after page, while they grope for the central focus or conflict, usually finding neither.

Now suppose you have figured out what the characters want from each other, right here and right now. The next question is: "How badly." How badly do they want it?

There is only one answer if your scene is to capture one hundred percent intensity: *very* badly. Every dramatic scene must be infused with a sense of want/need and importance.

If a dramatic scene is about people who want something from each other very badly, then a dramatic scene can be thought of as a battle. The next question to apply to the dramatic scene is: Who wins? The answer can be this one, that one, neither, or both. The point here is that the writer and reader, and the actor, too, must understand what's going on here. Battles have winners and losers, and sometimes draws.

But a note of caution here. Resolve anything in a scene without creating new conflicts, and the scene is over, and, more often than not, so is the movie.

Visual cues

What does each character *do* that shows how emotions are flowing in the *subtext* of the scene, or that shows *discoveries* are being made in this scene. What I mean by "do" is a physical rendering of feelings, a clear action that belies an unseen emotion. I will call such actions Visualized Emotional Cues (VECs) to separate them from the normal descriptive passages in a screenplay (we will explain this concept at length later in the chapter). Also ask yourself what each character is doing that belies nothing. Answer that with the Delete key. That falls under the category of the writer "puppeteering the actor."

Drive In/Drive Out

How can this scene be joined to the one before and the one after? A good screenplay has each scene "drive in" and "drive out." Scenes begin and end at points of dramatic tension, not at resolutions, tableaus, or entrances and exits. This way the writer maintains a forward momentum in the story. The only scene that resolves in a screenplay is the last scene.

Genre

What kind of movie it it? How is it using visual grammar? *Where,* meaning, "in what location" can this event happen for the best effect? By best effect I mean: best genre effect; best entertainment effect. What is significant about this place and these people? What is it that we see on screen? What is "genre" about where you are and what you are doing? What could be genre?

Two people sitting in a restaurant talking could as easily be sitting in the score board at Wrigley Field. Same people, same dialog. Would it be more interesting if they were in an airplane or a boat? On horseback? Ask yourself where is the most interesting, entertaining place to locate a scene. Your first impulse may not be the best impulse, so always question what you are doing. Get into the habit of second-guessing yourself.

Some definitions of terms

Subtext is that which is not written. It is that which is understood, or is happening between the lines. You cannot put two human beings together in a room without creating a subtext. It is simply the kind of species we are.

An example of subtextual dialog:

                    JOHN
      I'm having a party at my
      place tonight. Would you
      like to come?

                    MARY
      Do you want me to come?

                    JOHN
      Well, I thought you might
      enjoy it.

                    MARY
      Are you going to be
      there?

You can see these people are not talking about a party.

Discovery is a realization of something that has existed all the time but that the character never knew. It is when a subtext becomes text. It is the way conflict turns in a scene, meaning that when a Discovery is made the scene changes direction or ends. Discovery through conflict is the way, and should be the only way, exposition enters a movie (with certain genre exceptions).

Example:
                    JOHN
      Can I have this ring?

                    MARY
      I'd love to give it to
      you but I can't.

```
                    JOHN
          Please. I must have it.


                    MARY
          I can't. It was given to
          me by my aunt Mildred.


                    JOHN
          You have an aunt Mildred?
          So do I!
```

You can see that while in pursuit of some other need, John makes a Discovery. This, as opposed to John walking in and telling Mary he has an aunt Mildred.

There are genre exceptions to the Discovery guideline. When doing a "caper" movie, or a detective yarn, it is part of the genre to have someone walk in and lay down the case, the Objective, to the Main by just saying it. "I want you to find my missing husband. He has all the money." Discovery takes on a new dimension, with the change in Genre.

The Facts are implied only by what is happening in the forward momentum of the moment presented onscreen. THERE IS NO OTHER DRAMATIC WAY TO PUT FACTS INTO THE PAGES OF A SCREENPLAY. No exposition, no backstory, nothing that derails the story for the sake of what-happened-way-back-when that brought us to where we are. The genre exception of caper or detective story also applies here.

Dialog is one of the ways characters have of fighting for what they want from each other. It is nothing else. If a person does not want anything in a movie, he or she has nothing to say. When a scene provides information, color, tone, history, it does that only as a byproduct of people wanting things from each other and fighting for what they want in that moment, right here, right now.

Visualized Emotional Cues are essential to conveying the Subtext. Characters must *do* things in the scene that show how emotions are flowing in the Subtext, or that Discoveries are being made. These actions should come on the scene beats (any event that changes the direction of a scene), or at places in the scene where discoveries are made. Punctuate these beats with little visual cues, actions the character does, that show us how the person is feeling deep down, rather than oblique, non-visual statements of mind, such as "he flies off the handle" or "she's angry."

Proper use of cues on the page separates the novice's work from the professional's as quick as anything else. (For an in-depth discussion of this tricky topic see *The Scene Rack* later in this chapter.)

Human nature and scenes

American movies, and the scenes that comprise them, are about people in relationships. To write a good scene, a writer needs to grasp the basics of human nature: What is a person? What is a human being? What is a relationship?

Much of the understanding of human nature comes from experience and intuition, and cannot be taught. However, writers can benefit from organizing their insights into a framework.

For such a framework you might try reading the work of A. Maslow, an American psychiatrist, who set out, in his writings, to define the healthy human being.

Maslow developed what is called the needs hierarchy. He drew a pyramid and divided it into three sections. On the base level he put survival needs, meaning life and death situations: food, shelter, sex--that sort of thing.

The core of the survival drive is the need for safety and security, or in other words, the search for a home. Maslow maintains that a human being cannot strive for higher goals until survival, safety and security are assured.

Once survival is assured, humans advance to the second level: the need for Love and Belonging. The majority of people in the United States live on this second level of need.

"Tell me that you love me." Everything we do is a struggle to get love, respect, and admiration, in some form expressed from somebody. We are always trying to get someone to love us.

The core of the second level is esteem and self-respect: *"Tell me why you love me."* If I know you love me and I know why you love me, then I will feel good about myself and I will feel like I belong. This is practically a never-ending search. If you look around at relationships you will find that almost everything everyone is doing is in pursuit of acceptance. We even compete to be, or to be perceived as, the most loved, the fastest, the smartest, the best...which all translate into: *"Tell me that you love me."*

The third level at the top of the needs hierarchy is what Maslow calls self-actualization, which means to fully realize and express oneself.

The core of the third level is aesthetic knowledge, which is a sort of connection with a higher awareness, with the universal Human mind, or with some god or other. We cannot really become self actualized until we have climbed the two lower levels of the pyramid. We must feel truly loved and must have attained self-respect, which means we have already reasonably ensured our survival. Only now are we ready to go ahead and try to become what we really can be, to extend our potential outward. A self-actualized person often comes off as arrogant or rude, because they are fine with or without your approval. They also don't make good movie characters, because they are no longer in conflict with the world or the people around them They've resolved too many things.

Your characters are most likely going to belong on the second level, in the never-ending search for love and belonging. Before you start writing, try to determine how your characters define their underlying needs, and how they go about searching for love.

Remember, though, that love in the abstract is never the explicit Objective.

We can assume that because our characters are human, their ultimate objective is to find love and be loved. All scenes, all human interactions share a subtext of love or need: *"Tell me that you love me, tell me that you need me,"* or *"T need you, I love you, you must feel the same about me."* That's how it is, deep down in all of our interactions. **But no one ever says it.** It's kept subtextual. So, for the writer's purposes, the Objective should be simple, concrete, and three-dimensional.

Character motivation.

There are only two motivations: Redemption or Growth. In anti-hero movies or dark movies, a character will be motivated by self-destruction, (opposite of redemption) or self-denial (opposite of growth).

Know whether your character is motivated by need or

want. She could be searching for something because she has a void to fill (redemption). Or, she could be searching because she needs to grow as a person (growth).

The Universal Human Mind

Let us discuss a concept of particular importance to new writers. I call it the Universal Human Mind, and it is synonymous with a writer's (and hence the writer's characters') access to human emotions. Imagine, if you will, the entire universe in a box, our universe visible in its entirety from the vantage of a different dimension or a higher awareness.

The area within the box corresponds to human potential, to all that can possibly be felt, thought, or done.

Each individual human occupies some portion of the Universal Human Mind, but none occupies it all, and one or all people can occupy the same area.

Visualize humans as shapes inside the box. A person is like an amoeba, changing shape from growth in experience and awareness.

To some extent, my portion of the universe probably overlaps with everybody else's in America. However, other people have had thoughts that I have never had, and perhaps I have done things that other people have not done, so while we each overlap, we also retain our own uniqueness.

The point is that all of the universal human mind is *available* to any human, given the right circumstances. Anyone can be anything that any other human being is or has been. We each have the full potential of humanness, and so do all the characters in a screenplay.

Let me take it a step further. In the universal human mind, there is a vast palette of emotions: love, hate, fear and so on. We can conceive of it as being only *one* love, only *one* hate, only *one* fear. In other words, love is love, hate is hate, fear is fear. We all feel the same love, the same hate, and the same fear. *All humans possess all things human.*

All characters also possess all awarenesses and all potential awarenesses on all standard cultural levels. Do not have an American interracial couple dating each other in a small conservative town and have them not understand why people look at them strangely. If they live in this country they have to understand the rules of the game or they are not going to ring true. Your characters know everything you know.

Also, just like me and you, your characters are completely capable of doing anything that any other human has ever done. Your characters have needs. Your characters have wants.

> *The characters feel the same emotions*
> *that all humans can feel and*
> *they are capable of feeling all of them.*

Any limitations your characters have are something that *you* invented, and restrictions you put on them, and they will quickly reduce your characters to one-dimensional, life sized cardboard cutouts.

So, now, let me ask you a question about a character in a movie: Could the character ever consider suicide? Could the character ever be driven to murder? Could the character love that other (disgusting) character? The answer to all of these questions, and all others like them, is always "Yes." Properly motivated, all humans can do all things human.

Relationships in a Movie
Human relationships in a screenplay turn on the loves

and needs of the characters, and how badly they want what they want.

When writing, ask yourself: "What are the stakes?" Not only what does each person want, but also "how badly does he or she want it?" It is the writer's job to create relationships of love and need, and I mean the expansive Maslovian definition: "Tell me that you love me, tell me why you love me."

Without love/need there is no conflict. Defining the love in a relationship will lead you to the conflict, and it is the heightened love in relationships that heightens the drama.

Relationships are expressed through interaction. On some level, all interaction is **manipulative**. In a manipulative interaction, one person does what he does to evoke a certain response out of another. The reason they do this is to get what they want, so interaction is manipulative. The word "manipulative" has a negative connotation, but all your characters, good or bad, are either going to be manipulative or boring, self-actualized bumps on logs. It is far better to make them manipulative.

Interaction is also frequently **competitive**, which again comes down to trying to prove that you are more worthy of love than the next person.

Interaction can also be **nurturing**. Parents nurture their children in a totally selfless manner (in a perfect world), but all too often, it seems, we can see parents who use their nurturing love as a way to manipulate their children. It's not a perfect world.

Interaction can also be neutral, but, invariably, neutral interaction is boring. Do not create neutral relationships. Agreement kills drama. Keep your characters manipulative, competitive, wanting and needing. Keep them always driving for something, seeking out the love/need relationships, always with the stakes as high as possible. How badly do your characters need what they need? Well, very badly. The more they need it, the higher the dramatic value, the more entertaining the interaction, and the more you have of what's absolutely necessary to create a successful a movie.

Importance

Creating believable individuals in relationships of conflict is a good start, but it is not enough. Your third task as a writer is to question the importance of what your characters are pursuing, and the importance of the story you are telling from moment to moment.

> *Reality is the poorest excuse*
> *for bad drama.*

Nobody cares about what really happened, especially if the moment you are seeing on the screen is filled with endless, boring, but accurate, detail and dialog. This is a movie. Make it important. Forget about real. Forget about the boring, detailed reality of everyday life. As Lajos Egri said in *The Art of Dramatic Writing*, even a farce is better when the writer has something important to say.

Interesting people live their dreams, which, most often, conflict with their realities. (That's why they're dreams.) Why do people write spec screenplays? What are your biggest dreams? What are your characters' biggest dreams?

DIALOG

Dialog may be the least important single aspect of a screenplay, but it is where you will be judged, and where most of the changes will be made. One reason is that the people who will affect your script (producers, directors, actors), are not trained writers and dialog is the easiest, most obvious place for them to stick their barbs. Which doesn't mean there aren't at least a couple of producers or studio executives out there that can turn your gobble-de-gook screenplay into Academy Award material.

Dialog sometimes comes easy and sometimes does not, but you will be ahead of the game if you remember that the best definition of dialog in a movie is: "One of the ways people fight for what they want."

That is what all dialog does. It does not tell story and it does not give background, except as a byproduct. It is a tool used in the pursuit of a goal. It is used by the character only, not by the writer, or the writer's pedantic voice will soon be the only thing on the page.

Now, in the course of this fighting the characters might make some Discoveries. From such Discoveries the audience perceives some facts and background, but no character ever talks just to inform the audience.

Keep in mind that scenes are sharpened by judicious use of words and blunted with too many words. We are seldom as clever as we think. Spare the audience your witty dialogue and get your characters in conflict and fighting for something important to them. Seek out and express the conflicts in a scene, and always end a scene before an agreement. Agreement resolves conflict, and if there is no conflict there is no drama in the scene. That goes for comedy, too.

Always start your scene at the highest level of intensity possible and get out before it ends.

Do not let the characters ever say what they mean until the extreme moment of Discovery comes, and sometimes not even then. Human beings are wonderful for avoiding direct confrontational statements. We shade everything. We say what we do not mean and that is what makes a scene.

Let the reality lurk beneath the surface. Screenplays live in the subtext.

In Dialog,
Never ask a question,
but if you do,
Don't answer it,
but if you do,
Lie.

I've put in a little diagram called The Scene Rack. It is a representation of the structure of a scene and how that structure is presented in page formatting. Note that the "clumps" of dialog are interrupted with Visual Cues of the subtext. This represents the beats of the scene. A beat is any change in the way a character pursues the same thing.

In a properly formatted scene, the dialog is used in pursuit of some immediate objective. As the person speaking exhausts the possibility of getting the objective that way, he will switch to another strategy to get the objective. That is a beat. It works like this:

> JOHN
> Give me your pen.

> MARY
> No.

> JOHN
> Really. Give me the pen.

                    MARY
        No

                    JOHN
        Mary, I said GIVE ME
        YOUR PEN.

                    MARY
        No.

John goes to the window.

                    JOHN
        I'll give you fifty dol-
        lars for it.

                    MARY
        No.

                    JOHN
        A hundred?

Two things to look at here. How long can John go on asking for the pen before he changes his beat? Probably 5 to 7 lines back and forth max. When he goes to the window (the Visual Cue), that indicates to the actors and director when the change in beat occurs as he now shifts from the asking beat to the bribing beat.

Too many Cues will confuse the actors as to where the beats fall and sometimes cause the actor to misinterpret the scene. Too few Cues will have the same effect. Apply Cues incorrectly and the actors will spend half an hour trying to find the flow of beats which is something they should be

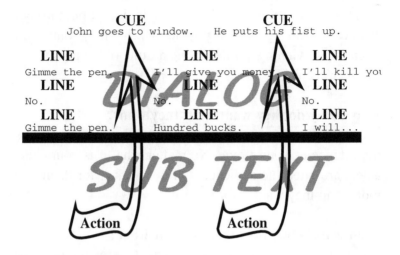

able to see on their first cold reading.

Questions to ask of any dramatic scene:

Be tough on yourself here. No one else is going to tell you. And don't assume anyone else even knows this stuff. Most of the development execs in Hollywood are about six months out of college. They're not stupid, they just don't know script from Shinola yet. Make it your job to know bad from good, and if it's bad, how to fix it.

What do they want from each other, right here, right now?

This is core of dramatic conflict. Remember the "want" is always defined in the other person. If A is talking to B about what he wants from C, then you have a "scene *about* a scene." The real scene should have been between A and C, so go back and create it.

How are they fighting for it here and now?

This is the "moment" of your movie. Lay it out through the beats of dialog as they grapple for what they want from each other, winning a little, losing a little, or having to start all over again.

How badly do they want what they want?

Only one answer to this: very, very badly. This is the importance of your movie. No matter what it is your characters are after, the audience will not want it for them any more than they want it for themselves.

Who wins? One, the other, both, neither?

Scenes are struggles to meet needs. One or the other or both or neither is going to get they want. This is not to be confused with Resolution. The characters do not resolve when they win or lose, they go on to their next need.

Is there drive out?

Drive Out equals Drive In to the next scene. This is the Scene Drive of your movie and is what keeps the pages turning. More a matter of technique than structure, make sure nothing resolves but their pursuits bleed over into the next page. It's the drive that continues from scene to scene.

Is there a Text vs. Subtext established?

The most boring screenplays have no subtext. The characters walk around like brass bands exclaiming themselves and their needs to anyone who will listen. Make sure characters never speak their truths until intense, extreme moments. And once spoken, those truths, discoveries, realities, will establish a whole new subtext between them.

Do they play their opposites?

Characters not only never speak their truths, they often speak the opposite of their truths. This is a big issue between men and women, and between people altogether. The man is in love with the woman and he wants nothing more than for her to stay with him, but instead he shouts "Get out of here!!" He "plays the opposite." Actors will often do this in the way they choose to play a beat, quite independently of or even in contradiction to the way the dialog has been written.

Are there Visualized Emotional Cues on beats?

What do one or more characters DO in the scene that shows how emotions are flowing in subtext, or that discoveries are being made in the scene?

A Visualized Cue looks the same on the page as standard action, stage directions, description, (or whatever you want to call the instructions written at the first left hand margin on the page). I call them Cues because they cue in the actors and director as to what the subtext is between the people speaking. They are not necessary to set the scene, as the normal action does. Rather, they reveal subtext and beats by their content and positioning on the page.

What is genre about the scene? What could be?

You cannot overdo genre. Can a comedy be too funny? Can a horror picture be too scary? Genre is carried primarily in the way things look, which is generated by where and when things take place. Genre is the most important aspect of marketing screenplays. Know the genre you are working in and know it well.

There is a difference between clear genre and cliche. Pay attention to what is happening in movies and, while exploiting the rich genre possibilities, avoid doing things the same way as other pictures. For instance, avoid the "phone booth in the rain breakup scene" in your Romance.

THINGS TO REMEMBER:

The facts

The facts are implied only from what is happening in the forward momentum of the moment presented onscreen. THERE IS NO OTHER DIRECT MEANS OF PUTTING FACTS INTO THE PAGES OF A SCREENPLAY (except with the previously-noted genre exceptions). All background, exposition, information, tone, mood, color, etc comes as a byproduct of the pursuit of needs.

The dialog

Dialog is one of the ways characters fight for what they want from each other in the moment. Fighting for what they want is also how they convey their feelings without ever saying their feelings. DIALOG IS NOTHING ELSE. Anything else that comes by way of dialog comes only as a byproduct of this conflict.

Dialog can be for entertainment purposes only but remember when you do that, you are stepping outside your story, and often what you think is a clever passage stops the forward Drive of the scene and movie for the duration of that dialog. Stepping outside the pursuit of the character's objective in order to do a little softshoe for the audience is fine and acceptable, but only when it works, and it works best when the softshoe itself is actually in pursuit of a subtextual objective.

Compare the "chatter scenes" in *Pulp Fiction*, *Good Will Hunting*, and *Fargo*. They all work.

The characters

What does each character want? What does each character *really* want? Work with the multi-level aspect of humanness. The more at opposition they are with themselves, the better. In a truly amateurish script, the characters all march around saying what they mean. The second part of this question is: How badly do they want what they want?

What does each character say about him or herself? About the others in the scene? Look over the dialog in the scene. What do they actually say? Pull the lines out and list them separately character by character. Do they infer a story by themselves?

If the scene is too long, the conflict is not focused on needs in opposition. Do not start writing the scene until you can answer the questions: What does A want from B, what does B want from A that they cannot have right here, right now?

If a speech is too long, the scene is underdeveloped in terms of meaningful interaction between thinking, needy people. Refer back to the previous question. Then take those brilliant long speeches and throw them out.

Entertainment value

Don't forget the reason movies exist. Scenes can be for entertainment only. So, can you have something that has nothing to do with anything that's just there because it is damned entertaining? Yes.

THINGS TO FORGET:

Exposition

A scene is never expository. It is never building up to something. It is never waiting for something to happen. It is never dropping down from anything. It is never holding a point in the structure because structure says it needs to be there on that page. Get rid of all that thinking. There is no exposition in a screenplay. There is only Discovery through conflict.

The job of a scene is not to explain what happened way back when. Scenes are in the moment. They are right here. They are right now. They are built on dramatic conflict.

Making certain things happen on certain pages

Everything that happens in the screenplay happens as the result of everything else that is happening in the screenplay. My best advice to the "page pointed" writers is: Cover up your page counter when you write. Write freely. Forget about the page counts.

WRITING FOR YOUR PRODUCTION COLLABORATORS

A scene is written for many different professionals in the movie industry. They need different information from your scenes and it is your job to write for them. At the same time, endless descriptive detail will make you no friends.

Writing for Actors

You have to be able to write scenes that are going to attract actors to the project. Actors like to come out and tear at each other. Give it to them. Let the people in your scenes feel more than one emotion at a time. Consider alternate interpretations of the characters' motives, because your actors will.

Actors also like to work with what they call a third point of focus. They like something else going on in the scene besides dialogue. They like to be in the kitchen, driving, or on the job. They like to be busy in interesting locations doing interesting things so they are not faced with black pillars of unrelenting dialogue.

Writing for Directors

Directors care about the visual aspect of a story. If your movie could just as easily be a radio drama, it is not visual. Make it uniquely and necessarily a movie.

Give the director opportunities to interpret your vision. Give them three-dimensional characters open to alternate interpretations. Give them a rich tapestry of visuals and events. Directors will love you for that. And they'll hate you telling them where to put the camera and how close.

Writing for Producers

What's the poster going to look like? What movie stars are going to want to play these parts? Is it castable among the big stars? What's going to hook an audience to come in? What events from the movie would go into the coming attractions trailer?

This is where the producer lives and this is what he is thinking. Above all, he or she wants to know the genre. Genre equals audience. Genre equals budget, equals advertising, equals everything.

Writing for the Crafts

Legions of people work from the screenplay during preproduction and the making of a movie. Oddly, most of them will never read it through for story or entertainment. These are highly vectored folks who have a job to do and want to be able to get in and get out with the information they need.

Remember that sluglines should not carry the narrative. They should be geared for budgeting and location work. Do not annoy a lighting professional with a slug that reads "LATE DUSK" or "CONTINUOUS." Tell them DAY or NIGHT so they know how to light without having to consult an almanac. Keep it straight, simple and to the point. Be kind to the crafts. And don't insult them. For instance, no set decorator needs to be told what props go on a desk top. Only describe things that are out of the ordinary.

Screenplay is a form of writing that no one wants to read. It's a means to an end. People are paid to read them, for goodness sake. Of the zillions of names that you see go by in the credits, very few of them read the screenplay start to finish to get what it's about. It really does not matter to them what is in the screenplay, except the specifics that pertain to their jobs.

People make entire careers at the scene level. The craft people and the actors live in the scene, not in the script. Remember them as you write--if not in the first draft, then as you polish your script for market.

SIMPLIFICATION OF THE PAGE.

Every screenplay is written from **four distinct elements**. They appear on the page in certain places in a certain rhythm. The four elements are: slugline; descript; dialogue; visualized emotional cue.

#1. Sluglines. Unless you are already an outrageously successful screenwriter, include only three items: INT or

EXT (interior or exterior); the name of set or location; whether it is DAY or NIGHT. The slugline tells the production people whether they are working on a stage or a location. It provides a name for the set or location on which the scene is to take place, and it indicates whether to light for day or night. The slug is in all caps and is placed at the first left-hand margin, also known as the descript, or action, margin.

#2. Descript. I use the word "descript" to refer to what is often called **Action** or **Direction**, or **Stage Directions**. I call it Descript to separate it from Visualized Cues which look the same on the page and are ordinarily bundled in with "Action" but have a different function in a script.

Every scene requires Descript at least under the slugline. That first line of Descript under the slug MUST contain the name of every character who is in the scene when the scene begins. Descript is used to describe the entrance and exit of characters when that occurs and any significant action happening in the scene. And, as mentioned before, the crafts need to know what they have to provide. General guideline: less is better. But that's it. Leave the thoughts and feelings out of Descript and write only what can be seen.

#3. Dialog. What you want the people to say, is put into a column about 3 1/2" wide on the page. Try to keep your ordinary individual speeches (sides) of dialogue down to three lines or less across that column, or a max of about twenty words. This will help speed the pace of the scene. This is not a stage play. If you are writing a movie that takes some additional entertainment value out of long speeches, then disregard the 3-lines-across guideline.

#4. Visualized Emotional Cue (Cue). I will use Cue to refer to the type of Stage Direction that describes through an action of the characters something the character is doing that indicates the character's subtext in the scene. These Cues are to fall on the beats of the scene, that is, whenever a character changes the way in which he is fighting for what he wants, eg: beg, bribe, threaten, cajole, etc. Typically beats and, hence, Cues show up every three to seven sides of dialog or so. Beats do occur frequently in a scene.

Screenplays live in the subtext. A screenwriter does not have people speak their subtext or tell the subtext on the page. A screenwriter doesn't write: "She is angry." A screenwriters writes: "She throws a flower pot through the window." The latter is a Cue because it is visualized action that shows how she feels. Couple that action with a line like "Yes, Darling and I love you." Which carries the meaning in the scene? The line or the Cue? Actions speak louder in a movie.

This is how the "beat and sequence" rhythm of a scene develops. It parallels the way characters are fighting for what they want, and determines the look of a page. A reader should be able to glance at a page from across the room and get a feel for the pace of the script without reading a word.

Get used to thinking about the four elements of a screenplay page: slugline, descript, dialog, and visualized emotional cue. They each serve a specific purpose, and the writer must know what they are as well as when and how to use them. That is really all you need to write a screenplay. Keep your pages clean and simple and your story will have an easier time shining through.

Sample of the four elements in a scene:

```
INT RESTAURANT - NIGHT          (SLUGLINE)


The  place  is  crowded.  Security  guards
stand  at  all  the  exits     (DESCRIPT)


AT THE COAT ROOM                (MINOR SLUG)


John gently touches Mary's hair.  (CUE)


                JOHN
        Keep  an  eye  on  the  reg-
        ister, Mare.


                MARY
        Yes sir.                (DIALOG)


She walks way without looking at him.
                                (CUE)
AT THE REGISTER                 (MINOR SLUG)


Mary slips a hundred dollar bill out
from under the drawer of the till
                                (DESCRIPT)
```

   INT   RESTAURANT - NIGHT is the slugline. It doesn't matter if there is a period after INT, or a dash before NIGHT. Number of spaces between them is also insignificant. Just don't underline it or number it.

   AT THE COAT ROOM and AT THE REGISTER are minor slugs. You can also use a minor slug to say things like "CHARLIE enters," in which case you are subtly calling for a close up on Charlie without actually writing CLOSE UP or CU.

You could also write "THE HUNDRED DOLLAR BILL has the code on the back" to call attention to the bill without calling for a specific shot. Let the director call the shots, and the writer denote visual emphasis in the scene through minor slugs.

Margin settings for format

If you want to start writing pages in your current word processing program, then start by setting two sets of margins. These are important, but there is not a single standard. Some writing courses want to make a career out of page formatting but it is very simple to apply.

There are two basic margin settings: an outside left margin, which we will call the descript margin, and an inside left margin which we will call the dialog margin.

The descript margin is easy to remember and acceptable if you make it "two and one": two inches from the left edge of the paper, and one inch from the right edge. The wider left margin allows for the binding. 1 3/4" is also commonly used for the first left margin.

The dialog margins are indented an inch from the descript margins, so they would be "three and two" inches from the left edge of paper and the right edge of paper respectively.

The character names for the dialog go on their own margin, one inch indented in from the dialog margin.

You will need to learn a few more formatting conventions. All pages are justified left only. Page numbering goes upper right. Font is to be Courier 12 point, or New Courier 11 point. There are no triple spacings down. Put only one space after a period everywhere. A completed screenplay should have fifty to fifty five lines from the first line to the last line (including skipped lines).

There are places you can call to buy scripts, but be careful since the rules of formatting change over time. Do not model your formatting on a script that is more than year old. You can buy *African Queen*, but if you wrote like they did, it wouldn't fly today.

Then again, you can simply buy a screenplay formatting program. If you don't have such a program, get one. They all do pretty much the same thing, more or less, are all interchangeable, and all cost about the same. When people ask me what I recommend, I always say, "whatever's on sale." Packaged screenwriting software is becoming more than a convenience to a screenwriter. Producers are using scheduling and budgeting programs designed to interface with screenwriting software. Choose a program that runs well on your system and is sold by someone you trust.

Sometimes writers want to ask that a certain transition between scenes be done in a certain way. At one time, CUT TO was used as a transition between every scene, but this practice is largely out of favor today. Transitions go flush right on the wide margin between scenes in CAPS. Some Transitions are: FADE (meaning FADE THE PREVIOUS SCENE TO BLACK AND FADE BACK IN AGAIN ON THE NEXT SCENE); WIPE (meaning ONE SCENE IS WIPED OFF BY ANOTHER MOVING ACROSS THE SCREEN ALA *STAR WARS*); MATCH CUT (the previous scene matches the visual or sound of the next); INTERCUT (cut freely back and forth between the two scenes); SMASH CUT (an edit for jarring effect)... ultimately, if you become famous enough, you can do whatever you want there.

New writers misuse these things to death as soon as they learn about them, so if you are new to this, don't use them. The one transition that is that handiest is INTERCUT, most often used when a phone call is happening and you want both onscreen locations, cutting from one to the other.

Things not to do

Do not number your scenes;

Do not direct the camera (use minor slugs instead);

Do not direct the actors (use cues instead);

Do not write CUT TO between scenes;

Do not underline slugs;

Do not use any artwork;

Do not refer to "we" in a screenplay as in "we see..." or "we hear..." (we'll assume if you write "Birds sing" that we can hear them);

Do not use parenthetical asides to the actors to tell them how to read a line;

Do not capitalize the names of characters in descript after their first appearance.

Chapter Ten:
REWRITE
Story Diagnostics
Common problems with scripts

STORY DIAGNOSTICS

The Sag Line

Once you know *why* things work the way they do in a screenplay -- *why* it has a three act structure, *why* there is a Character Structure, *why* there are Drives in operation, *why* resolutions come about -- how these specific and knowable elements create certain specific effects, it is possible to trace a problem in a screenplay backwards from its effect to its cause in order to determine what is wrong and how to fix it.

The Diagnostic Ruler below can be invaluable in finding and fixing problems in a script created by Structural errors (as opposed to page-level or scene-level screw ups).

Imagine yourself reading a script. Suddenly you begin to think of other things that you absolutely must be doing right now - like scrubbing your tub, arranging your sock drawer, or alphabetizing your spices. Note the page number of the script you are reading. The number will be your guide for tracing the problem back to the writing error that created it, many, many pages earlier.

The origin of a problem often goes back a long way, because it takes time for the drives to develop. It may take

Anatomy of a Screenplay

FI 30	31 60	61 90	91 FO
Problems in the setup come from a lack of clarity in the Character Structure. Do not begin until you know your Character Structure.	If the problem is here, the main Drives failed. Look to Decision and Event. Event usually before 45, Decision usually after 45.	If the script sags here, the Opposition is either missing or inactive. Also check the flow of the story beats *vis-a-vis* Character Structure.	A problem in the third act means the script has had a premature resolution or loss of structural characters and/or Objectives along the way.

20-30 pages after an Event happens for the desired effect to occur. The opposite is also true: a missing Event will take twenty pages before the reader senses that something is missing. By knowing how drives develop in the different areas (character, story, etc.), and knowing on what page the problem surfaces, you can trace the problem back to the cause.

Problems often seem to come out of nowhere, but they never do. Beginning writers, producers, and development executives will most often concentrate on the area of the script that is sagging, treating the symptom rather than the cause.

1-30

If the sag hits in the first 30 pages, the writer is writing about things other than, MC, Obj, Opp, WC, Event, Decision, Theme, and Genre. The writer is probably laboring under the mistaken notion that exposition belongs in a screenplay, or that everybody cares what happened in the past, or that dialog can exist for its own sake. If the movie falls apart by page 30, the writer does not understand the movie s/he is writing and must go back to the starting point (Story Line) to make decisions regarding Main Character, Objective, Opposition, and so forth.

30-60

If the sag occurs in the second 30 pages (between 30 and 60), one or more of the drive elements failed to kick in.

If the sag is on pages 30-45, lack of Story Drive is usually the problem, and so Missing Events are the cause. If it sags between 45-60, it is usually because the Main Character has made too few Decisions (Character Drive) or none at all.

For example, you are reading a script titled "The Woman Who Couldn't Speak English" The Main Character is a woman who cannot speak English. She is taken in by well-meaning people who make a fuss over her. They react in strange ways to this beautiful, fragile newcomer. By page 35 you are dying to get back to alphabetizing your spice rack. There has been no Event outside the Main's control, and hence, no Story Drive. By page 50 the unmatched socks in your sock drawer are calling to you. This is a Main Character who makes no Decisions, and who gives us no Window into her mind. There is absolutely no Character Drive in what must essentially be a character piece. You, and every other reader (except the writer's mother) will never get past page 35.

60-90

If the first sag you encounter is between pages 60-90 the

reason is almost certainly under-developed or inactive Opposition. We know in a movie that a Main Character is pursuing an Objective. We know that in order to keep the pursuit interesting over the 2 hours required in a feature film, it is necessary to provide Opposition to this pursuit (or to change the Objective from time to time in an Episodic Narrative). If there is no Opposition in a single-Objective movie, or if the Opposition disappears, the movie will sag, and it will always sag between 60 and 90, and sometimes earlier if your other Drives are not well established. The reason is that an interesting Character in pursuit of an interesting Objective only stays interesting for about an hour without Opposition or change in Objective. Then tedium, and the trips to the zoo, inevitably sets in.

Example: the Main Character's kid is kidnapped in an attempt to force the Main Character to say where the money is hidden. The kidnappers set off with the boy and hide out in the mountains. The Main Character frees himself from the police to pursue his boy. And so he pursues. Good stuff, so far. But by 65 it is sag city. What happened?

When the kidnappers take off for the hills, they, the Opposition, effectively have been taken out of the movie. The bad story analyst or rewriter will try to fix the problem on page 65. The good story analyst or rewriter will go back to page 25, where the kidnappers first took off, and attempt a fix starting there. The writer can either give the Opposition something more to do in the movie, (hopefully with or to the Main Character), or the writer can introduce a new source of Opposition. The point is that once the sag can be pegged to page 65, everyone can identify what the problem is.

90-end

Should the sag show up in the last quarter, that is, somewhere after page 90, the problem is always that one of the Structural elements of the movie, (or more), as set up in the first thirty pages, has already been resolved. The Third Act is merely a mirror image of the First Act. Either resolutions have come too soon (the Main Character and Opponent joined forces on page 82 or something), or structural elements have been lost along the way, or they were missing to begin with, (although if the problem is missing structural elements, it will show up long before the Third Act).

If the script will not resolve in any satisfying way, the most likely reason is that all or part of the Character Structure has already been resolved. Unbeknownst to the writer, the movie already ended back there, but s/he keeps writing because there are more pages to fill. While it may seem emotionally satisfying to have Harry marry Sally on page 62, the resolution must be been saved for the ending, unless you know a place to sell a 62-minute movie.

Another reason a movie refuses to end is the introduction of characters and objectives along the way that are working outside of, or against, the central, original Character Structure. When it comes time for convergence, the damn thing just dribbles on and on.

COMMON PROBLEMS WITH SCRIPTS

The following are mistakes common in screenplays. Even a professional's first draft will include some. If you are a developer or a reader, watch for the patterns that emerge based on the categories below. The categories will suggest ways to make a poorly executed but good idea more manageable by making corrections on a global scale, by category, rather than on the scene level.

If you are a writer, you must learn to be your own toughest critic (probably not possible because there are some really tough critics out there waiting to slaughter you). Look for problems in your script by assuming you have them all. Writers are too quick to approve their own work, leaving the problems for the readers to point out. Assume you have all of the following problems, search into your work to find them, then plan to do lots of rewriting.

REALLY DUMB GOOFS

Under this heading come the mistakes that will immediately embarrass a script. They include but are not limited to:

Page Formatting. Mistakes here are just plain aggravating and can be fatal. Common wisdom is: If a writer does not know how to format a page, he or she does not know how to write a script. The guidelines are available everywhere, in books and in software programs. Page formatting is the easiest and most obvious thing to teach in screenwriting classes, so is the most common thing taught.

Be advised that the standards of page formatting evolve over time. If you doubt it, pick up a screenplay from the forties and see what you find. Make sure your standards are current.

Page layout/shape. Just as a story progresses through beats and sequences, so does a scene. You know you are in the hands of a pro when you can look at a page without reading it and know the pacing of the scene. (Refer to chapter nine on Scene.)

Proofing. Proofread before and AFTER YOU PRINT anything. The computer spell check function is not enough. I
would recommend that you get someone to proof your
script for you, because the writer often can't see the mis-
spellings, incorrect words, or typos, even when they are
pointed out.

Character line. This refers to the line above the dialog that
indicates which character speaks the line that follows. So
many mistakes are made here that this problem deserves its
own heading. Make sure that the character's name is always
the same throughout the script. After a rewrite, make sure
you haven't changed lines of dialog while forgetting to
change the corresponding character lines. There are no double spaces after Character Lines. See also, Hanging
Character Lines.

Slugs. Sluglines do three things: they separate the INTs
from the EXTs, they name the set or location, and they say
whether it is lit for DAY or NIGHT. Anything else in a slug
is experimental writing and should be avoided.

Make sure the same sets and locations are referred to by
the exact same names throughout the script. A slip here
could add to the projected budget, or label you a novice
writer.

Some writers like to say CONTINUOUS where DAY or
NIGHT should go. This can sometimes help the reader keep
the continuity of a given sequence clear, but, more often
than not, is a pain for the reader and the people who are
going to break down the script for budget and schedule.
What I recommend is that only if the writer feels CONTIN-

UOUS is, for some reason, necessary should the word appear, and then only *after* DAY or NIGHT in the slugline. Also, don't say DAWN unless the you can see the sun coming up in the shot. Stick with DAY or NIGHT and you won't go wrong. eg:

EXT SCHOOLYARD DAY (CONTINUOUS)

Adding the parens around the CONTINUOUS makes it easier for the reader, etc, to pass through it.

Hanging slugs, character lines, and speeches-- A hanging line occurs when the slug appears on one page and the accompanying descript is on the next, or when the character line is stranded by itself at the bottom of the page, with the corresponding dialog on the next page. Never separate a slug and its descript or a character line and its side of dialog.

If you must write a long speech and it has to break at the bottom of the page, put "(more)", centered in the dialog margins, and then, on the top of the next page, write the character name again and put next to it, in parentheses, "(cont)", or "(cont'd)," to indicate the speech began on the previous page.

BEAT AND SEQUENCE

On the story level. Every scene fits into the Beat and Sequence structure of the screenplay. When a script runs out of steam, the writer tries to invent things for the characters to do that have nothing to do with the original storyline or objective. Here is the dead giveaway of a bad script, and I jokingly call it, a "Trip to the Zoo." (I call it that because, for some unknown reason, the zoo seems to be the most common destination for characters whose story drive has dropped dead.) The story drive is collapsing (or never began), but yet here are all these blank pages that have to be filled up with *something...* what's a poor writer to do? Well, a surprising number of writers pile the cast into the car to go to the zoo, or to the ballgame, or to visit friends--or just cut to a montage with bouncy music. Montage is French for : *Your story drive just collapsed.*

On the scene level. You know you are writing or reading a bad scene when the dialog takes over and spills into the next page and the next page and the next... A scene where people talk and talk and talk. Characters in a movie don't talk, they fight for something from each other. It only stays interesting when the way they fight is constantly changing. Each change represents a Beat in the scene. The lines that work out that beat form the sequence and carry the scene to the next Beat. Typically a scene sequence lasts three to seven lines, and then comes the next scene beat. Without this rhythm the scene fails to develop any drive and collapses into wonderfully pointless dialog. Usually endless pages of talk.

CHARACTER MISTAKES

Pre-Introduction of Main Character. Remember that the Main Character and your movie are one concept. Any prologue must respect the integrity of your story. Anything that happens in a movie before the Main Character appears still needs to relate somehow to the Main Character.

Character Introduction. Make your characters' first

appearances count. The audience is actively processing every bit of information they receive from the page/screen. They will assign volumes of information to each new character and try to fit each one into the overall matrix of the movie. Too often a writer will introduce a character without giving the audience enough to digest.

When a movie begins, the audience immediately starts looking for who the Main Character is, so they can take part in the story. Give it to them. Make it clear. Make the Main Character's first appearance be a metaphor for the person he or she is, or an allegory for the journey he or she is about to undertake.

Example of Main Character introduction:

```
FADE IN

Slow fade on the beautiful face of a
teenaged girl, MARY JO GRAY, squinting
into the last few strokes of her makeup
job, perfect chestnut hair flowing past
porcelain skin.

One look in the mirror of the vanity
confirms she's done, but she doesn't
smile. This is a face that doesn't
often smile.

INT   MARY JO'S BEDROOM - DAY

The heavy drapes are pulled tight so
only hints of the sunlight outside can
squeeze through.
A sad-faced stuffed mouse watches from
```

the vanity as the makeup tools get packed into an oversized shoulder bag.

Her MOTHER is there, too, looking out of place.

> MOTHER
> One more smart word out of you and you're not going. I don't care if it is a school trip.

The girl picks up a spray can of face lacquer and sprays it across her face. She still hasn't looked at her mother yet.

> MOTHER
> C'mon. Let's go.

Mom leaves the room, carrying the suit-case.

Mary Jo, seeing she's gone, quickly pulls a styrofoam head with a wig that matches her own hair from under the vanity. She stuffs it into an overnight case.

She picks up the sad-faced mouse and gives him a special kiss. She gently wipes off the lipstick mark she made.

> MARY JO
> I didn't want to have to
> do this, but I've made
> up my mind.
>
> MOTHER (O/S)
> Move your butt!
>
> MARY JO
> I'm going and I won't be
> back. You'll have to
> take care of the others.

She puts the mouse in the array of stuffed animals on her bed.

She turns her back on the room and snaps off the light.

Emotions. This is where you, the writer, will live or die. Feature films trade in human emotions. When characters deal with each other on an intellectual level, the movie dies. When they deal with subjects that do not inspire emotion, the movie dies. When the writer approaches the job as an intellectual exercise, forget it. The characters' emotions must be full and immediately accessible.

And remember, people do what they do because of how they feel *now,* not because of what happened to them at some other time and place.

Integrity/motivation. Bad writers want to control the reactions of the characters rather than do the difficult thing and let the characters react in ways that are honest to what has come before. Manipulation of the characters to achieve something the writer wants is a terrible sin against the audience. Manipulation of character to meet a writer's pre-ordained page-pointed event schedule is just as bad. Keep your characters motivated by what is happening *in the movie and at the present time* and let them follow their own paths, and take their own journeys, no matter how much of a writing problem that may create for you.

Change/Growth. Audiences come to see extraordinary things happen to characters. That's the only reason why their story is being told in a movie in the first place. So many bad screenplays trudge through a series of events with no one changing, growing, or becoming any worse for the bother. This is especially true of first screenplays, which too often ramble through vaguely autobiographical sketches that no one but their author understands.

Lack of Sympathetic Characters. A common problem is that no one likes the Main Character or any of the other characters, and neither the reader nor the audience would invite any of them over for a barbeque. Write a script about unlikeable people and you will have an unlikeable script. Things that make Mains unlikeable: cheats on loving mate, kills innocent bunnies, etc.

Do it vs. Say it. Bad scripts rule this category. ANY TIME people in the movie are talking about what happened, or what is happening somewhere else, the script is in trouble. ANY TIME the action to which they are responding is something we have learned about through conversation, the script has a problem. ANY TIME one person is talking to another about what he wants from some third person, you are on the edge of losing the audience. ANY TIME the movie becomes about something that did not happen in this movie, on the screen, your audience will become annoyed or bored, or both. Keep the movie in the moment and on the screen.

Disappearing MC. Typically, every scene in a movie either includes the Main or refers to the Main. A common problem is for another character to enter the film and take over while the Main Character disappears for ten or twenty pages. Sometimes the writer will follow the Window Character down blind alleys and "to the zoo" because the writer finds the Window more interesting than the Main. In such a case, it may be better to go back to the beginning and switch the Window and the Main Character.

Consistency in Action/Reaction. The content of any scene is affected by the preceding scenes. If your action hero is badly beaten up on on page 23, then on page 24 he better have a bruise somewhere and not be doing gymnastics in bed with the babe. This sounds self-evident on the surface but probably only because I am using such an extreme example. All too often characters are manipulated by their page-pointed writers to get the desired reaction for the needs of some plot. The characters must be free to react in the same way any human would react who has had the same cultural biases, educational experiences, and self-motivated drives.

Integrity in Action/Reaction. The sequence of Action/Reaction must correspond with the reality created within the screenplay, whether the writer likes it or not. Integrity refers to the truth of the person and the honesty of any flow of actions. As Aristotle put it "Be consistent in your inconsistencies." This has a profound effect on how the script is perceived. The script will establish a premise, presupposition, proposition, or somehow lay out the reality of the world in which the script lives. This implies a "level of reality" operating within that world. For instance, *Superman, Taxi Driver,* and *The Little Mermaid* each inhabits a different world. Too often scripts feel free to combine reality levels and almost always to the detriment of the movie. It is also true in screenwriting that FORM EQUALS CONTENT. The screenwriter, once the form is established, must stay with it.

MC is not the mover. The Main Character is synonymous with the movie, and, therefore, the Main Character moves the story with every decision, discovery and action s/he takes. The action or flow of the movie must remain centered on the Main. If other characters are making major decisions the audience will attach to them or just be confused as to whose story you are telling. There will be cases where this is the desired perception. A movie like *Terminator* has the big bad robot coming to kill an innocent woman. The story follows the woman's desperate flight to evade demise, and so you might argue that she is the Main. But she makes few decisions of her own. It is the Terminator who is running the movie. It is not unusual that a Main exists only in his or her reactions to the Opponent.

Wooden Character. Look at your Main Character and make sure you understand the reason he or she acts a certain way. My suggestion is that once you are sure you understand it, try *changing it* and see if the new motivation brings your story to life a little more. Remember, ten people can do the exact same thing, but can give you ten entirely different reasons why they did it. It is one of the wonderfully interesting things about humans. This changing of motivation will present new possibilities. While it is true that all humans are capable of all things human, the only thing that stops or starts us from doing something is Motivation. Properly motivated, ANYONE WOULD DO ANYTHING.

Motivation. In a potential universe of all human emotions and actions, some people will do one thing and another person will do another thing. What separates them is motivation. Know that humans are motivated in one of two ways: out of deficit (need, lacking something, something needs to be put right, etc.), or out of growth (challenge, adventure, growing up, etc.).

Trying to motivate the Main Character to do something with exposition or backstory rather than through discovery is just bad screenwriting. In other words, the Main Character is out for revenge because of something that happened twenty five years ago. Yes, it's deficit motivation, but it's emotionally removed from the character by time, and makes for lousy movie writing. The Main Character needs to be motivated by something that is happening right now in his life. Remember: everything in the moment and on the screen.

Wishy-washy character: As opposed to wooden character, a big problem in scene writing is omission of characters' wants. Without wants or objectives, scenes amount to nothing more than small talk. Even if all you have is two people standing at a bus stop together, you must understand that on some animal level the man wants the woman to worship him, sleep with him, or at least like him, and the woman wants the man to love and adore her, or take her away to a rose covered cottage. A person who wants nothing in life is a one dimensional character, nothing more than a puppet or a cardboard cutout, that is wasting space in your screenplay. Get rid of him or get him an Objective. Make sure you know what everyone in your screenplay *wants* and I mean everyone.

Lack of Conflict: Conflict does not mean "fight". Conflict means needs in opposition. Here is a scene of tremendous conflict:

```
INT   BEDROOM   NIGHT

John and Mary are making love.

          JOHN
     I love you.

          MARY
     I love you, John.

          JOHN
     Run away with me.

          MARY
     I can't. I can't leave
     my kids.
```

Please notice there is no fighting going on here, no guns. As a matter of fact they are making love. They have tremendous needs in each other that they are unable to attain. This is the real meaning of conflict. Too often scripts resort to mindless battling with guns and fists to conjure up conflict where none exists. Probably the reason why so many chop-socky and wham-bang action movies are almost totally devoid of any emotional involvement with the audience.

Creating and/or Expanding on resolutions instead of the conflicts is another mistake under this category. We care about the conflict, that is, continuing needs in opposition. When the conflict has come to its highest point, cut to the next scene. Only one scene in a screenplay requires resolution, and that is the last scene.

Boring Main Character. When other characters are, or become, more interesting than the Main Character, you need to stop and reconsider. A student gave me a story line once: "It's a movie about a kind of an accountant-type guy who goes to the wake of his friend and he goes there and he comes up to the coffin and is looking down at his friend in the coffin and all of a sudden his friend in the coffin winks at him." Well of these two characters, which would make the more interesting Main Character, the accountant or the guy in the coffin? It's the guy in the coffin.

Main Character as Martyr. The totally selfless Main Character: "Everything I do, I do for you. I sacrifice everything for you and then I die, and you'll never ever be able to repay me." I thank one of the network programmers of family programming for this one. She deals in a lot of "suffering mom" stories and she once said to me that martyrs may have a place in our literature but not in our movies. Always know that your characters perceive their own self interest in every situation. Even if the character doesn't know it at the time.

DIALOG

This is a large category so I've broken it down into the following subheadings:

Text vs. Subtext. The error here is in lack of subtext, which means that characters come right out and say exactly what they mean, or do exactly what they say. One of the keys to understanding human behavior and, by extension, movies, is that we never say what we mean. We are always after something, trying to prove something, trying to do something other than what we seem to be after, proving, or doing.

Good writers will set off what a character says in the text against what we know he really wants in the subtext, and then when the truth of the character collides with his own denials, a great Discovery of self takes place. This can happen an unlimited number of times in a movie.

Screenwriting must be executed in such a way that the potential of the subtext is fully expressed. All of dramatic scene work-- scene structure, dialog, genre, description and cues--revolves around this key question: "What are they *really* after?" If the writer does not know what the characters are really, really after, deep down, scrap the scene.

Here is an example of text vs subtext. What is going on here in this conversation in a donut shop between young Lisa, 15, and the donut man, Paul, 45?

```
INT   DONUT SHOP - DAY

Lisa sits at the counter. Paul comes
over.

                PAUL
      Merry Christmas, young man.
```

                    LISA
        Happy New Year! How are you
        going to celebrate?

                    PAUL
        Doin' nothin.' How 'bout you?

                    LISA
        No school for two weeks.

He touches her book.

                    PAUL
        What are you reading?

                    LISA
        World History.

                    PAUL
        A school book?

                    LISA
        From my honors class. I love
        history.

                    PAUL
        What happened to your
        boyfriend? Did you make a
        date? Where is he today?

She flashes anger.

                    LISA
What boy!!?

                    PAUL
Woah. I'm not a cop. I"m just
trying to make conversation
here.

                    LISA
What boy?

                    PAUL
You blew me off yesterday to
talk to someone else. Was
just wondering if you got
anywhere.

                    LISA
Oh, Ronny. No. Nothing.

She crosses her legs.

                    PAUL
You have to be careful with
these boys... but you know
that.

                    LISA
Well... Ronny is sweet
enough...

                    PAUL
Did he hit on you?

                    LISA
No. He's just a boy.

                    PAUL
Well, that's the idea.

                    LISA
I usually try to find controversial topics to discuss,
but they're... I don't
know...

                    PAUL
Not into it?

                    LISA
These fragile boys can't take
a little uncertainty in their
world.

                    PAUL
I used to argue controversial
topics with customers in
here, but no more. They have
such destructive beliefs.

                    LISA
Destructive beliefs?

                    PAUL
Self-destructive, I should
say.

```
                    LISA
      The notion that they alone
      possess Truth? Gets old fast.


                    PAUL
        I know. So I shut up

  She looks directly at him.

                    LISA
      So, what are your beliefs on
      sex with minors?
```

Lisa, an impatient child, pulls the subtext up to the surface with a big splash. Once that happens, either the scene ends, or takes a 90-degree turn as a new subtext is established.

Writerliness, or Seduced by the Words. Bad writers often get caught up in their own cleverness and write word plays, or beat metaphors to death in dialog between characters. We are seldom as clever as we think. The reader and the audience would rather you spared the wit and told the story.

A text-heavy script identifies an amateur faster than anything. The pages are black and heavy with photocopy toner. A screenplay is an airy, bright breezy read, typically 175 to 200 words on a page. Avoid the long speeches, avoid the big black blocks of descript. Say what needs to be said, say it only one time, say it clearly, with as few words as possible, and move on.

Example:

```
INT    BEDROOM - DAY
```

```
Patterned wallpaper covers the walls.
Against the wall by the window is a
wooden stand upon which is mounted a tin
wash basin with a pitcher. Next to that
stands an armoire, clothes haphazardly
hung from the open door. An area rug is
half under the bed, half out. MATT
BOUDREAU, a handsome lad more inclined
to sports than study, in his early twen-
ties, is asleep under a sheet.
```

compared to:

```
INT    BEDROOM - DAY
```

```
Early 1920's decor. MATT BOUDREAU, 23,
is asleep under a sheet.
```

It is conceivable that writerliness might carry a script through two hours. Heaven bless all such endeavors. I prefer screenplays that deal with story.

Redundancy. Writers have a tendency to repeat things, to say them more than once, to be redundant. Do you see what I mean? Do you get it? Understand?

In the rewrite class at the The Screenwriters Group in Chicago, participants are asked to cut six pages of dialog only. The assignment is often met with incredulous howls and sighs, and later laughed at when writers find themselves cutting 10 or even 20 pages in redundant dialog alone.

```
INT    CROWDED AIRPORT - DAY
```

It is busy. Holiday travellers pack the concourses and gaterooms. Frantic travellers vie for position in long lines. Tempers flare as patience with harried passenger agents wears thin. CHARLES GEYSER, 32, pushes his way through the thronging humanity.

How many times did the sample above happen to mention the airport is crowded? (Don't forget to count the slugline.) One will do, thanks.

Dialog Dependency. Bad dialog can take many forms, but without a doubt, Dialog Dependency is the number one problem in bad dialog.

Dialog must not state or confirm events in the movie. Dialog does not give backstory, set scenes, tone, show anything, tell facts, except as a byproduct of its primary function. Dialog: one of the ways people fight for what they want from other people. Many, many things happen in movies without ever being spoken. Hitchcock called dialog "background noise." A movie is NOT the sum of its spoken words.

Questions in dialog. Ok, here is Dan Decker's handy dandy Rule of Questions in Dialog: Never ask a question in dialog, but if you do, never answer it, but if you do, lie.

One idea per side-- Dialog is most effective when it is terse and to the point. Generally, one idea suffices for each speech or side. Avoid:

>   JOHN
>   I will not give up till
>   I escape. Then I will
>   come back and rescue
>   you, darling. Then we
>   will move away. We can
>   have some children. We
>   will buy a condo...

Better to stop at the part about escaping.

No conflict. Conflict is needs in opposition. When there are no needs in opposition, there is no conflict, no drama, and nothing to talk about. If you have dialog, you had better have something the people speaking want from each other. Even when it is tempting to have a character say something to "show the audience" how he's feeling, the script must make sure it is said in the pursuit of a need.

MISTAKES IN STORY NARRATIVE

Narrative flow. A screenplay tells its story in the way scenes join one to the next. Story is what the audience never actually sees, but understands from watching the sequencing of the scenes. If the scenes do not show a clear path, the audience is lost and the story the writer wants to tell fails to materialize, regardless of what's in the individual scenes. Story does not happen under a slugline. It happens *across* them.

Missing scenes- Extra scenes- Transitional scenes- Every scene in a screenplay fits into a sequence. Look at each sequence to see that just the right number of the right scenes are in place, and this whole piece of the puzzle fits. How do you know when you have it right?

1) Approach the work as if you did not know what it was about.

2) Why is this an exciting enough story to make a movie about?

3) Choose the scenes as if your life depended on it.

Write and/or leave in only the *good* scenes. If you have any doubt, cut. If it is your absolute favorite and you absolutely love it, cut it because you've lost your objectivity.

Sequencing. Sequencing is the blood pressure of your screenplay. If you have too many or too few sequences, the pacing of the piece will be off. Sequence is the series of scenes that follows a Beat. A beat is any Event, Decision, or Discovery that changes the *way* in which the characters pursue the *same* objective. Action pictures have more beats, three to five pages apart; dramas have fewer, five to seven pages apart.

If the scene you are reading or writing does not fit into a sequence that has arisen from a beat, what is it doing in the screenplay?

Understanding this structure within a screenplay requires that you disengage from the scene level and stand back for an overview. Readers should get into the habit of noting every time a beat occurs so they are able to put their finger on this pulse. Writers will often draw up a "beat sheet," a list of the beats of the story. This can be used like a table of contents to help find their way around the manuscript.

Drives. Drive is what keeps the reader turning pages, and what glues the audience to their seats. The Rack lists six common Drives in American movies: Objective, Story, Character, Theme, Genre, Entertainment. With a little imagination, the writer can concoct and develop unique Drives. A screwball comedy can develop a Stupidity Drive. The audience is spellbound by the stupidity. A horror film can have a Grossness Drive. People will stay to see the next gross thing.

It is when the screenplay collapses into scene after scene of no connected or compelling interest that the Drives go away, and so does the reader and the audience. When the scenes answer questions or give information it's death to Drive.

Coincidence. Avoid having your story rely on coincidence. How did they meet? "Well, they, um... bumped into each other! yeah! that's it! they literally bump into each other! It could happen." Coincidence thus becomes a great big writer's convenience, and characters are smashed into each other by the writer, who has yet to create three dimensional characters that would meet and be motivated by who they are.

When it works, Coincidence is a device best reserved for comedy, even better for farce-level comedy, but only when coincidence itself becomes a humor metaphor or driver of the laughs. Example: The early farces of the eighteenth century playwrights, and right on into the twentieth century, relied heavily on coincidental meetings. The more coincidence you could pile up, (accidental meetings in the drawing room, mistaken identities, etc.), the funnier they became. In a film, however, (that typically has a higher level of reality), coincidence will work against the reality.

So, yes, it could happen, might have actually happened, but not in a movie. Each event or decision must grow plausibly out of the last. Coincidence is neither Story nor Character, and it is not a Drive element. Better that an accidental meeting turns out to have happened not really by chance at all, but the result of two characters being Driven to the same place at the same time by their own needs, (rather than the needs of the writer), then your movie reality is safe.

Too Fast Too Soon. The writer, the script, the reader, and the audience must revel in the telling of the story. "Boy meets girl. They fall in love. They make love. Okay, now, on page two...." The writer knows where the story is going and does not want to give it time to get there by itself. The story of a relationship, (and all movies are relationships), is a "dance". It goes like this: He takes a step toward her, she takes a half step back, he steps back, she steps forward, he steps forward again, she...

Often conclusions of the most brilliant order are reached from evidence of the slightest weight. All movie ideas are winners and all movie ideas are losers. The difference is in the telling.

A Trip to the Zoo/starting new movies. As mentioned earlier, a trip to the zoo occurs anytime the story, character, or any other central drive collapses. So what happens? Everyone piles into the car and goes to the zoo, or goes skating, or goes to Paris, or the movie cuts to a snappy montage to bouncy music. The writer has to do something, because the central drive train fell off its rails.

A lost writer will often add a brand new character and then will have lots of new scenes that have nothing to do with what the movie was about before. This amounts to starting a new movie, and the cause for it is the same as for a trip to the zoo.

A movie is the story of the particular set of characters you start with, doing the thing they've set out to do, and ending up in some way. Each beat and sequence of the movie deals with the pursuit of this. Writers who forget this get lost and in their desperation to get something, anything at all, happening, will take their characters to some new place in hope something interesting will magically happen to them.

Example: ET comes to earth. Befriends the boy through an elaborate dance. The bad guys are looking for ET. The boy has to find a way to get ET home. The bad guys show up at the house. The boy takes ET to the zoo, doesn't phone home. Bad guys go roller skating. Mom finds a new boyfriend. Alien mother ship arrives, wonders what happened to the movie. And where the audience went. Fortunately, Melissa Mathison, the screenwriter of ET, didn't get lost, never went to the zoo, and called home.

Lack of variety. Changes in the way people pursue the same thing are crucial to maintaining interest in a scene, story, and movie. It is what Beats are about. "Please may I have it"; "Give it to me or I'll kill you!"; "I don't want the damn thing" are three variations on the same goal. There should be a change every three to seven lines in dialog and every three to ten pages in story, depending on and defining pacing.

Genre Violations. Once a writer has established the genre, the script must be told in that grammar. I am not saying you cannot have a funny moment in a drama. I am saying you should avoid a car chase in a family breakup movie unless you have a bomb-proof reason for including an action genre set-piece in a heart-felt drama. Or worse yet, say you're doing a comedy like "Wag the Dog". It's the story of some guys who try to save the upcoming election for a President who just molested a child in the oval office. It's an extremely funny, satirical piece about manipulating the pop culture. So say the characters somehow succeed in saving the President, but then, for some reason, the Main Character is killed in the end to keep the secret. This might well be considered a genre violation and a kick below the belt to an audience who thought they were coming to see a comedy.

BACKSTORY or "What really happened". My personal favorite setup for backstory in a bad script is "So tell me, Fred, what *really* happened?" Such a line is always followed by a page or two recapping the last twenty years in Fred's life that brought us to this particular moment.

There are some other lines guaranteed to evoke an eye-glazing response: "Tell me, Otto, don't you miss the old country?"; "It's nothing. You just remind me of someone I knew." "Do you remember your first time?"

Here's the rule: No one cares. And after you delete it from your script, no one will ever miss it.

Overwritten. The soul of screenwriting is brevity. There's hardly a first-draft screenplay written that cannot be cut by twenty pages without losing content.

That Explains It. This is the reaction of anyone watching a movie where information is given off the screen. That is, dialog that answers questions; scenes that "show" things; backstory; explanations; exposition; etc. Once the information is given, the audience can say, "Well, that explains it," and get up and go home. DO NOT GIVE INFORMATION FROM THE SCREEN.

Poor convergence. This is the pay-off of what the screenplay spent the first 30 pages setting up. Once the beginning is written, so is the end. The third act is the first act in reverse. Problems with the ending are always in the beginning. The Main Character is surrounded by a structure of characters and it is that Character Structure that converges on the last page of the screenplay.

Four things need to be accounted for: The relationship between the Main Character and the Window Character; the Objective; the Opponent; the Theme. No convergence means the audience walks away unsatisfied.

If the story will not converge, it means that either the story lost one of the structural characters (moved away or died) along the way or one of the resolutions of the convergence has already been resolved (on page 81 or so). This commonly happens when the Main attains his Objective too soon. When that happens, even if it's on page 60, the movie is over. Once the Main Character gets the girl, wins the Objective, vanquishes Opposition, the movie is over.

DRAMATIC SCENE

Beginnings and Endings. The "Honey, I'm home" scene opening coupled with "Goodbye. Goodbye and thank you. You're welcome. Goodbye." scene ending has stopped more stories cold than anything. This is a movie, not a play. Scenes do not have to start with ENTER and end with EXIT. Start each scene in the middle of whatever is going on and end at the peak of the conflict, before a resolution, and your scene will "drive out," that is, the audience will be straining forward, looking for a resolution, and their forward momentum will carry them into the next scene.

One of the best ways to stay on target with the beginnings and endings is to know the "moment before" the scene actually begins onscreen. Use that as a springboard into the more heightened dramatic level that exists somewhere in the middle of conflict. Don't write the moment before, just know it and see that the scene flows from action already in motion.

A much less common problem, but a problem nonetheless, is the reverse situation, when a scene is too compact to contain the conflict. Just be aware that a scene must breathe and flow between the actors, the visuals, and the writer. The writer has to lay out colors on the palette for the audience to paint with. The writer must watch for the opportunity to include the things that audiences like to see in scenes, that actors need to work with, and that directors want to visualize.

Dramatic conflict. There is a little mantra every screenwriter must learn to chant before he or she writes a dramatic scene: "What does A want from B that he cannot have right here right now, and what does B want from A that she cannot have, right here, right now. And how badly?" If you cannot answer this question, do not write the scene. The movie exists only in this moment on the screen.

If a character is alone on the screen, the writer must clearly know what the character wants, period. Once another character is on the screen, too, then their wants and needs are defined in that other person.

DESCRIPT (also known as Action, Direction, Stage Direction)
There are only two kinds of descriptive writing in a screenplay. One describes what is seen on the screen:

```
Joe gets out and goes to the mailbox
with the letter.
```

The other, while also describing what is seen, exists for the purpose of showing what characters are feeling. This is the Visualized Emotional Cue that belies the subtext:

```
Joe throws the flower pot through the
window.
```

Descript has no other functions. If you are ever tempted to include opinions, insights, proverbs, lyrical passages, or purple prose, remind yourself that the audience will never read them. Your movie speaks through visible action and dialog, or not at all.

Epic Descript. Limit your descript paragraphs to three lines and you will be forced into the proper economy. I once read a screenplay by a lawyer that ran on for nearly an entire page with a description of the inside of a courtroom. After 100 years of movies and 50 years of television, there's no one in America who doesn't know what a courtroom looks like. Just say COURTROOM.

This problem arises when the writer thinks that he or she is also the set designer. The set designer designs the sets. Let them.

Epic description can also create real-time problems. Bad example, (sluglines deleted):

```
John races out of the apartment to the
elevator, but the floor indicator stays
stuck on the sixth floor so he finally
```

```
races down the ten flights of stairs,
runs across the street to the conven-
ience store, grabs a bottle of wine, has
to wait for a chatty customer in front
of him to pay for it, then hurries back
across the street into the building only
to find the elevator still stuck on the
sixth floor. He runs for the stairs...
```

If the writer would simply take a stopwatch and time himself actually doing the action he's called for in one short paragraph, he'd find it eats up about 20 minutes and adds absolutely nothing to the movie.

Using Descript as Narration. Also known as Novelizing. For bad example:

```
Joe felt that throwing the flowerpot
through the window would make his
point. Deep down, Sam understood this.
```

No. Joe just throws the pot. A screenplay is not prose. A screenplay is not a literary vehicle at all. I think it would be possible to write an entire screenplay without a single complete sentence. Descript does two things only: tells what is seen on the screen and describes actions that belie subtext. Descript does not narrate or give information beyond character descriptions and relationships:

```
CHARLOTTE, 52, regal, Joan's mother,
appears.
```

Asking the impossible of the actors. This occurs when the

Descript calls for the characters to do something that is just plain impossible. If the reader or writer isn't sure, just put the script down and try to act it out. For bad example:

```
INT   MARY'S APARTMENT   DAY

John and Mary are making passionate
love, nearing climax, when there is a
knock at the door. They stop, he puts
his clothes on and answers it.
```

The writer ought to get into the habit of acting out the descript before writing it down for the actors. Try the actions on for size, ease, possibility, desirability. Do not force the actors to rewrite your directions on the set.

Unclear, missing, misplaced descript. This problem is less common than the excessive use or broad misuse of descript. Of course, it is possible to err on the short side. Descript must provide the critical information needed to keep the story clear, visual, and in motion, in the fewest words possible--and not a word less.

Puppeteering the Actor. When directions to the actor do nothing to reveal subtext but exist only to tell the actor when to move, laugh, cry, whatever, they constitute puppeteering. I include in this category *all* adverbial parenthetical asides to the actors, such as (angrily), (sweetly), and recommend that they not be used at all.

This also applies to scripts that punctuate every line of dialog with a line of direction to the actors in the form of a cue, creating a sawtoothed profile to the left margin of the page as it shifts back and forth between dialog margin and descript margin.

This problem, again, comes up when the writer mistakenly believes that he or she is also the actor and the director. This is not to say "never give a cue;" it is to say: let the actors decide when to laugh and cry and let the writer write a scene in which it is possible for them to do so -- a scene so laced with emotional subtext that the actor and director must feel the emotions on the page without the writer having to say: CRY HERE, PLEASE.

"How do we know?" This is a variation on novelizing. It is a common mistake.

```
The  cop  approaches  the  car.

                COP
         License, please.

Joe  hands  him  his  license. He  remembers
the  last  time  he  got  stopped.
```

Okay, so, "how do we know?" he remembers the last time he got stopped. And no flashbacks, please.

VISUALIZED EMOTIONAL CUES. Or just plain "Cues." This is how a good writer conveys the truth of the character to the reader. The Cue is the action that punctuates the beats of a scene. I will always separate out Cues from "Action" or stage directions, (which will simply be called "Descript"). The Cue is different from the regular descript passage because it's intent is to reveal subtext. For example:

```
                    JOHN
          Up yours!


                    MARY
          Bite me!


                    JOHN
          Go to hell!

She slaps him.
```

Compare to:

```
                    JOHN
          Up yours!


                    MARY
          Bite me!


                    JOHN
          Go to hell!

She laughs.
```

It's the same dialog, but has a totally different meaning. The truth of any scene is not in its dialog, but in its Cues. This is an example of when it is proper to use a Cue to direct the actor. When she says "Go to hell!" and laughs, which is true? Always the action.

For example, when Joe throws the flower pot through the window, it is safe to say that his interaction with other characters in the scene is changing. The Cue underlines the change. Alternately, Joe might say: "I love flowers," and then throw the flower pot out the window. So which is true, the line or the action? Always the action. Cues reveal the truth, the subtext and therefore tend to represent major events or decisions in a scene.

Missing Cues. This was always my biggest problem when I was learning how to craft scenes. I would leave out the action that revealed the subtext. Boy, oh boy, for ME the scenes were rich in subtext, roiling in human emotion... unfortunately I was the only one who knew it. There was a private movie screen in my head rolling the movie that I failed to convey onto the page. If nobody can understand your vision it is as if you never had one. Cues help you connect.

Improperly used/misplaced cues. A cue is an action that reveals subtext and falls *on the scene beats.*

Show don't tell. Cues are the solution to the problem of telling instead of showing. To show instead of tell, take it out of dialog and put it into Descript and Cues, thus creating three-dimensional visual actions that reveal the characters and their emotions and put the motion in your motion picture.

SETUPS AND PAYOFFS

Everything that appears on the screen must be "part of" the movie. If it is introduced onscreen, it must somehow come into play later on. This is usually spoken about in terms of "setups and payoffs."

Setup with no Payoff. Everything, EVERYTHING, that goes into an American film must be set up and then paid off in some way. In American films, everything counts.

Payoff without Setup. Then there's the opposite problem. It usually comes about when the writer gets a great idea on page 76 or so and sticks it in. It was never properly set up and comes out of nowhere, and leaves the audience wondering where the movie went without them.

REALITY CHECK

Improbability/inconsistency/believability -- you must be consistent within the world you've created in the script. This applies to all categories above, across the board.

ENDINGS

The mistake is made when the four main elements of the Character Structure are not resolved, or not resolved together, as the last thing before the FADE OUT.

Do not start your movie with one Main Character and end it with another (this is not as uncommon as you might think).

The Main/Window relationship is one of the core emotional elements in the movie. This must be resolved.

Resolving the Opponent means, simply, making clear what happened. Does s/he get their Objective? Does the Opponent survive? Go on to a greater glory?

Resolution of Objective means that the script must let us know if the Main Character got what he or she was after.

Resolution of theme means give us a sense of what is going to happen to the Main Character after the FADE OUT. What happens to this particular sort of person who goes through this particular journey and comes to this particular ending? The audience expects some message to come from the movie, and you can look on resolution of theme as the "moral of the story." Get it in there, because if you don't, the audience will make one up. The clever screenwriter does not let the audience write it.

PROPER PRESENTATION

When your screenplay is written, rewritten, reassembled, polished and proofed, pat yourself on the back, go out, sleep in, take a day off, do whatever you want to do to celebrate having come this far.

When you are recovered, copy the script on three-hole punch paper, and bind it with fasteners such as ACCO round head solid brass fasteners. Use two fasteners. I know it seems better to use three, but the industry standard and tradition is two.

Also get a heavier weight sheet, such as eighty-pound cover stock, to use for a backing. Adding a cover to the front is nice but not required.

Then make sure that on the title page, (although you can repeat the title page on the cover), you have included the name of the movie, "an original screenplay by" and your name. Towards the bottom on the left, write your name, address, and phone number. Cover letters are very often separated from the scripts. A lot of times when I need to contact a writer, I reach for their script and count on their number being there.

And while nothing guarantees that someone won't steal your whole movie, take one copy of your script and either register it with the writers guild, or copyright it with the government, or both.

IN CONCLUSION...

A lot of people write screenplays who probably shouldn't. A lot of people write screenplays who have absolutely no training or talent in the craft. Why this industry draws so many people who think they can just pull a screenplay out of thin air is a mystery. It is the equivalent of designing a building with no training in architecture. Rely on good training to put you ahead of the unwashed masses who are writing and submitting bad, unreadable screenplays all over the place.

Once a draft is "done enough" to be read, contact people who can give you professional, objective third party critiques--better that they do not know you and do not know your project and relate only to the page and nothing else -- that will give it to you straight in the chops.

Once your draft has been rewritten enough, (somewhere between 3 and 15 times?), consider entering it in one of a number of screenwriting competitions in America. They are designed to help you get attention; to get a little "heat" on the script. Every producer has a fantasy that out there somewhere someone is writing the next *E.T.*, just as every writer has a fantasy that there is a producer with a lot of money just waiting to buy the writer's script. How do you bring these two people together? The producer knows that 99 percent of the scripts written are not even worth the time it takes to read the first ten pages. So how do they find the ones that are worth the time? Well, some look toward competitions in the belief, correct or not, that the judges are going to knock down the dreck.

People often ask me what books I recommend for screenwriters to read. As a rule, I always recommend books that are written for the other disciplines involved in making movies. The writer needs to become an authority on everybody's business, because everybody comes to the screenplay for answers. Read books on directing, books on acting, books on producing, books on human psychology. Read anything by Joseph Campbell, who talks about the universality of story. Read anything by A.H. Maslow, who talks about what human beings really are and how they relate to each other.

To master the screenplay, like any other realm of human endeavor, we must first learn the fundamentals. Sometimes it's a long and arduous learning curve to climb before we can let go and engage the task joyously. As we master the organic, singular nature of a screenplay, we can actually feel it in our writing. Then we can let ourselves come forth on the page. Where training and instinct meet is where the best work will occur.